SINGLE-MINDED

Also by Cliff Richard:

You, Me and Jesus
Jesus, Me and You

CLIFF RICHARD

SINGLE-MINDED

Hodder & Stoughton
LONDON SYDNEY AUCKLAND TORONTO

Photographic Credits

British Library Cataloguing in Publication Data

Richard, Cliff
  Single-minded
  1. Pop music. Singing. Richard, Cliff –
  Biographies
  I. Title
  784.5'0092'4

  ISBN 0-340-48809-3 Hbk
  ISBN 0-340-48971-5 Pbk

Published by Hodder and Stoughton,
a division of Hodder and Stoughton Ltd,
Mill Road, Dunton Green, Sevenoaks, Kent TN13 2YE
Editorial Office: 47 Bedford Square, London WC1B 3DP

Photoset by Rowland Phototypesetting Ltd,
Bury St Edmunds, Suffolk

Printed in Great Britain by
Richard Clay Ltd,
Bungay, Suffolk

CONTENTS

INTRODUCTION

It's hard to believe that eleven years have elapsed since my autobiography *'Which One's Cliff?'* arrived on the bookshelves. I'd assumed then that the really eventful days were behind me. Twenty years in the business and I'd done it all. How wrong I was.

Nineteen eighty-eight marks my thirtieth 'showbiz' anniversary and possibly my one hundredth hit single. I've just completed two of the longest and most exciting concert tours of my career, my current album has 'gone platinum' and I'm as amazed as anyone to find myself still rubbing shoulders with the likes of Rick Astley and George Michael in national polls for 'Top Male Singer'. A few months back, I apparently became the first artist to fill Birmingham's huge NEC arena for six consecutive nights – and, year by year, life still seems to be gathering momentum. I can only sympathise with my press critics who, despite having dug my grave long ago, are becoming increasingly peeved that I won't lie in it. Maybe I'll keep them waiting a while longer!

People tell me I'm single-minded in the way I approach the things I regard as really important. I'm not sure whether that's a virtue or a weakness, but perhaps the book will help you be the better judge. In any event, I thought the title was pretty appropriate!

Enjoy the read, and my thanks once again to Bill Latham for making sense of my thoughts, to Gill Snow for making sense of Bill's writing, and to Hodder & Stoughton for making the book!

Cliff Richard

1 DOING 'TIME'

1 DOING 'TIME'

'You'll be bored out of your mind within six weeks,' they said. 'Six nights plus two matinées a week, the same lines to deliver, repetitive stage movements, the same old songs. Not to mention dragging in and out of London every day. The last six months will be a nightmare.' Great words of encouragement they were, as the days rolled by to the biggest theatrical project of my career.

What if these Job's comforters turned out to be right? It was all so new and totally different from anything I'd tackled before. Until then the longest concert tour I'd ever undertaken without a break was of less than three months. Admittedly, the old Sixties' Palladium pantomimes probably ran for nearer four, but I remember getting fed up with them long before February was out! What was I letting myself in for? The one consolation, if it all proved a disaster, was that I'd have the days free for tennis.

It's funny how things turned out. In fact I played far less tennis that year than I had for ages. Somehow the opportunities seldom cropped up.

Yet, despite that drawback, the twelve months from April 1986 proved just about the quickest period of my entire thirty-year career – and I loved every minute of it. Even thinking back now, many many months after I left *Time*, I still get a tingle down the spine, remembering the excitement and exhilaration of the whole thing. And there's even a lump in the throat when I think of someone else playing 'my' part.

Knowing what I know now, it was ludicrous even to entertain the possibility of boredom. Not for one fleeting moment was I bored, and I'm half-ashamed ever to have considered it.

There I was, doing all the things I most wanted. It had always been my ambition to star in a West End musical, and this was it. A combination of what I'd always done with what I'd always wanted to do. I was acting, dancing and singing the music I loved best, in a show that was sci-fi and stunningly different.

Perhaps it isn't too obvious what a total change it was for me to be part of a team of actors and dancers working in a play. In concert, which is my usual art form and which I understand inside out, you relate solely to the audience. OK, so there's the occasional rapport with the band behind, but basically you're communicating and relating exclusively out front, and throughout you are the principal focus of attention. Not so with a play. It isn't good enough to concentrate merely on what you have to say and do. That's easy, and if in a concert the mind goes blank, it's relatively easy to ad lib a line or two – even a whole chunk of a song lyric. It's amazing what garbled words I've sung on the spur of the moment to 'Living Doll' or 'The Young Ones' on occasions.

But lose concentration in a play and there's big trouble. Let your mind drift away for just an instant to what you'll be eating after the show, and something goes in your head and no one, but no one, can help you. It's your responsibility to cue the right line that will eventually put the dialogue back on course. Even if I ad libbed for five minutes, I'd still somehow have to get back to that all-important cue line for another actor.

Fortunately that only happened to me a couple of times and, I tell you, it's like a combination of every nightmare you've ever had. But it was a vital professional lesson, and even more important, it helped with something I'm probably not very good at in real life – that is listening to other people with real concentration. Like most performers, I do tend to rabbit on a bit!

Apart from the sheer enjoyment of *Time*, therefore, I guess it was the concentration factor that repelled any likelihood of boredom. If being bored meant losing concentration, then I was simply too terrified to get bored! Believe me, 'drying' on stage isn't an experience I'd recommend.

I can only assume that I'm lucky with the kind of temperament I have, for even if I haven't exactly enjoyed certain career experiences, I don't think I've ever suffered with what must be a crippling tedium. Elton John once said on a TV chat show that 'Cliff will go on for ever because he never seems to get bored.' I don't know about that, but I do know that if you throw yourself into something wholeheartedly your enthusiasm isn't only infectious, it's also self-perpetuating.

Of course there were occasions during that year in *Time* when I would have preferred to stay at home. There were the few days after Mamie Latham's death, for instance, and particularly on the day of the funeral. But I'll tell you more about that later. There was the August Bank Holiday, when I wrote off my VW Golf on the M4, and arrived at the theatre not quite knowing whether all of me was intact. There were the nights when I just didn't feel too good. There were two really bad bouts of sinusitis, I remember, when it was really painful to hit those high notes. But, strangely enough, the moment the music kicked off and the revolve started to turn for the opening rock number, every other feeling receded and I was able to throw myself into the plot almost automatically. My instincts reminded me that there were two thousand people out front, and no way was I going to let them know I felt bad. And once I started that was it. The next thing I knew, it was the intermission!

Whether you put it down to enthusiasm or not, I don't know, but I was almost paranoid about being late. Every day I was usually the first member of the company in, and after a while it got to be kind of a joke. Usually I was there at least an hour before it was strictly necessary, but I reasoned that, if for any cause I was held up, even for an hour, I'd still have forty-five minutes to get ready before curtain up. On the day of the car accident, I reckon my logic was justified. Even then we went up only twenty minutes late, and the audience wasn't aware there was anything wrong.

In any event, I enjoyed getting there early. I enjoyed the relaxed atmosphere and comfort of the dressing-room, which I'd furnished with several bits and pieces from home. I enjoyed getting the make-up on slowly, making a cup of tea, watching a bit of TV. It was a gentle process of becoming 'Dominionised'!

I'm also a bit chuffed with myself that I went through the whole year without missing a single performance. Actors tell me that they've never heard of anyone else going through a complete year without having some time off – so, as far as I know, it could be some kind of 'First'. *Guinness Book of Records*, please note! In fact I was daft, right at the outset of the project, not to have insisted on some kind of break during the run. Enjoy it though I did, there were times when I felt pretty clapped out, and a couple of weeks' holiday would have been great for recharging the batteries. I remember at the beginning of August my usual holiday-mates going off to the villa in Portugal for the annual bake-up, leaving me just a tiny bit aggrieved. Mind you, driving them to the airport was probably a mistake!

In all seriousness, I'm both thankful and amazed that my throat stood up to its daily pummelling. If my voice had gone, then that would have been it. I'd have had no option but to duck out. Yet strangely, despite the usual ration of coughs and colds, my throat seemed to be immune.

To omit any mention of holiday from the contract was a mistake. What was wise, was to exclude myself from the midweek matinée after six months. That afternoon performance really is a drag and seems to intrude right into what should be rest time. I felt slightly smug, I must admit, when, just a few weeks after I gave up the Thursday afternoon performances, they were cancelled because bookings became so few! Future producers had better register the fact that they won't get me for eight shows a week again. It's more than flesh and blood can stand – at least at my age.

Talking of records, by the way, I'm also led to believe – although I can't guarantee it – that we created some kind of attendance record. Apparently more people came to see our show in one year – something approaching three-quarters of a million – than had ever attended a single West End theatre in a year before. I'm well aware that this was largely because our theatre, the Dominion, was so big. Its two-thousand seat capacity is five or six hundred bigger than most, and several other shows, such as *Phantom of the Opera* or *Les Misérables*, would certainly have matched it if they were playing there. Nevertheless, I'm proud – justly, I feel – of our eighty-five percent capacity throughout the year. And it's certainly one in the eye for those critics who wrote us off so mercilessly at the beginning.

I suppose I was hurt by some of those reviews, but even more by people within the industry who seemed either to ignore us or to hint that we were intruding improperly into West End theatre's hallowed ground. Some months after I completed the show, for instance, one actress whom I've worked with in the past and whom I love dearly asked whether *Time* had given me a taste for 'proper' theatre. I think my face smiled, but inside it was more of a snarl.

Perhaps I was, and still am, far too defensive about *Time*, and of course I have to be biased, but to my dying day I don't think I'll ever understand why the show didn't receive at least a couple of accolades. Firstly, it deserved one for its extraordinary set. I can't believe that any set anywhere in the world has been more exciting, exotic and extravagant than John Napier's brilliant high-tech design. Goodness knows how many times I heard people say that watching the spaceship landing on stage was more spectacular and realistic than a Spielberg movie. And in the Ascension scene, the combination of lasers, lights and sounds produced gasps and sustained applause night after night. Yet in the prestigious National Theatre Awards' Design Category, *Time* wasn't even nominated, let alone a winner. On the other hand, a Gilbert and Sullivan show that was taken off after eight weeks and was dead and buried by the time of the awards ceremony, was there among the four nominees, and TV showed the customary clip from one of the scenes. To me it seemed pleasant, but desperately ordinary. John Napier wasn't mentioned. *Time*, apparently, was just a four-letter word.

Then, secondly, there must be someone among the West End's theatrical overlords who would have a word of praise for the undisputed fact that *Time* pulled audiences into a London theatre. That surely has to earn us a plus? I'm positive that eighty percent, perhaps even more, of the 650,000 or so people who travelled to the Dominion from all over the country – and some from overseas – weren't even occasional, let alone regular, theatre-goers. They'd know all about live concerts, for sure, and probably movies as well, but quizzed about theatre they'd be clueless. Now I believe some of that number will have had their eyes opened to the existence of another form of entertainment called theatre, and that it isn't reserved for the highbrow, the super-intellectual or the fuddy-duddy. Will someone, I wonder, grant us that *Time* may have broadened horizons and in doing so achieved a service for theatre, rather than having raped it?

If I sound cynical, forgive me. Maybe there were political goings-on behind the business scenes that I was happily oblivious to and that would help explain what to me is currently inexplicable. But meanwhile, I'm left with the personal and rather unsatisfactory conclusion that the world of theatre doesn't take kindly to nonconformists. It's the same in many walks of life: to be different is to court suspicion and unpopularity, and, if nothing else, *Time* was different – a first in many ways!

For a start, we took sci-fi as a theme and brought it to life on stage. When my sisters' kids said it was like going to see *Star Wars*, only for real, I thought, 'That's what gets up everybody's noses – we've done the impossible!' Sad though I am to say it, the theatre world seems to be entrenched in its tradition. If you don't conform to a three-act play, presented with a certain style of predictable lighting, in front of sets that are prone to collapse if the door so much as slams – sorry, it isn't proper theatre. No place for sci-fi. Perish the thought of lasers or flashing lights. And imagine Lloyd-Webber messing with vulgar rock 'n' roll!

As a cast we were realistic enough to know that we didn't have the best script in the world – but as a musical we were competing, and our set was out of this world. Perhaps that was the problem! We talked about it, moaned a little, would have been encouraged by being recognised by our fellow professionals as having a worthwhile role, but, at the end of the day, we got on with the job.

The team spirit and morale among the cast were incredible. Towards the end of the run we were going out together as a company after the show every week. Sometimes we'd order pizza and watch a midnight movie. Often we'd take over the local Greek or Indian restaurant and chat and laugh until two or three in the morning. For me it was all a very different lifestyle, and when it was over I missed it dreadfully. I vowed to keep in touch with everyone. And for a while I did, like you do after a holiday. But inevitably the good intentions waned and today I'm in touch with only a few. But I made some good friends and that experience alone was certainly enriching.

Somehow the casting turned out to be fantastic. Jeff Shankley as Melchisedic, and Clinton Derricks-Carroll as Ebony, the space pirate, proved perfect 'opposites'. But, over and above the character balance, we seemed to balance as people. I, for example, respected and was at first slightly in awe of Jeff's acting abilities, but learnt a tremendous amount from his generous advice and example. I like to think that he may have learnt a tip or two from me about singing techniques!

You can't go through a year like that without a few hilarious experiences. Like the night when, right in the middle of a critical piece of dialogue, a guy ambled down the aisle from the back of the stalls and, calmly as you like, clambered on to the stage. The stage crew in the wings and the security men out front were either asleep or frozen with shock, because no one moved to stop him. Slowly and deliberately the guy, who must have been drunk, drugged, or both, took off his jacket, turned to me, stood, and just stared. My line at the time was something like, 'I don't want the world to crumble away, but I don't see how I can stop it.' Automatically, I added, 'What do you think?' As if rehearsed, I got an answer. 'Try peace, man,' the drunk blurted. Around me I was conscious of the rest of the cast falling about with laughter, but mercifully by then someone had the presence of mind to come on stage and gently ease the intruder away. He went without protest. It was still my line. I snapped my fingers, and just said, 'As I was saying . . .' The audience erupted with applause, more from relief than anything else, and we were back into character again.

There was another night when I remember giving what I thought was a brilliant piece of acting. I'd just saved the world and had collapsed blubbering on my knees with every ounce of emotion I could summon. Suddenly I became aware of the three girls on stage almost beside themselves with hysterics. Seconds later there were stifled giggles from the audience. 'Can't people recognise an Academy Award-winning performance when they see one?' I thought. I glanced around the stage to see if I could spot the joke. I prayed that I hadn't split my trousers or worse! I didn't need to look further than Laurence Olivier's fifteen-foot sculptured holographic head.

Slowly, his eyes rolled right the way up from his chin, past his mouth, through the nostrils, and eventually settled somewhere slightly adrift of the eye sockets. I learnt later that the computer, which synchronised the projected film on to the sculptured head, had gone on the blink, and the film had actually started before the head was lowered into its correct position. As the head came down, the effect was to slide all the features gracefully from chin upwards. The best theatrical face-lift ever, they told me. Eventually I saw the joke!

In fact it was amazing just how little did go wrong, in view of the incredibly complicated technology that was involved. I'm not mechanically minded in the slightest, and it's all I can do to change a fuse, so when people asked me how those incredible effects worked, as they did most nights, I used to go on about there being thirty-two hydraulic moving parts and so many tons of this and that equipment, and hoped I sounded reasonably knowledgeable. Actually, you would have needed an honours degree in engineering to grasp the ingenuity of it all.

Yet, despite the show's advanced high-tech nature, we, the actors, never felt dwarfed or overwhelmed by it, and that, I guess, was also part of John Napier's wizardry.

My concert experience was also a great help in that respect. Many's the time I've stood on stage and been bathed in myriads of striking green beams as lasers are bounced off a revolving mirrorball. It doesn't upset me if people's attention is riveted on those effects for a while, for we are deliberately out to create a total impact, visual as well as audio. Adam Faith underlined it for me. He came to see *Time* one night and said that, despite all the stunning effects, he never stopped caring for the characters as people. That balance is important. John Napier knew that the effects must complement the actor, not obliterate him!

Again, it was an extraordinary achievement that, apart from Lord Olivier's shifty eyes, and a disaster early in the run when a massive piece of equipment dropped through the stage and caused a three-day cancellation, so little actually went wrong – which, come to think of it, is probably just as well. I hate to imagine what could have happened if, for instance, the platform on that enormous disc which upended itself on stage every night had failed to operate. It was an awfully long way to fall! Again Napier the Mastermind had it totally under control. 'Never mind how wonderful it looks,' he said. 'If it's not a hundred percent safe, it's out.' One little switch at stage right, marked 'Hydraulic power cut', would have immobilised just about everything, and any one of us was at liberty to push it if we sensed any kind of danger. No one ever did.

Precautions, too, were systematic and obligatory. Not once in 402 shows was the cast allowed on stage until every moving part had been checked and rechecked. Maybe it looked as if we were hanging on by our fingernails. In reality it was as safe as houses.

Having been around in the business for as long as I have, I'm fairly accustomed to meeting 'star' names, and in all honesty, I can't say that it particularly excites me any longer. When I first started out, I always kept an autograph-book handy and collected quite a list of celebrity scrawls. I've long since lost it, I'm afraid, having discovered that behind the reputation, however 'mega' it may be, there's a very ordinary human being, who goes to the loo and gets cabbage stuck in his or her teeth.

I can think of only one person in recent years who's made me totally and justifiably starstruck, and that was Laurence Olivier. The show had run more than six months before we met him. Only the technicians responsible for filming and modelling the sculptured head had had any contact with the great man prior to the show's opening, and on opening night itself Lord Olivier was too ill to attend. Everyone was bitterly disappointed, but there was some compensation for me by way of a personal telegram of best wishes. I framed it and it now has pride of place in my library at home, alongside the bronze bust of the actor's head on which the giant stage model was based.

I couldn't believe my bad luck when we heard that Lord Olivier was coming in. Of all performances, he had chosen a Thursday matinée – and I'd stopped doing Thursday matinées two weeks before. It says a lot for my understudy, John Christie, that he agreed to swap with me for that one show. Admittedly, I had his arm twisted behind his back at the time, and he still got paid! Seriously, I was grateful to John for understanding and, when the time came for cur-tain up, we couldn't have been more tense, even for a Royal Command Performance.

Lord Olivier was seated all by himself at the very front of the Circle. Midweek matinées are rarely well attended and on that Thursday we had spread the word around the fan club that we'd specially like an appreciative audience. They never let me down, and that day they were at their enthusiastic best.

Aware that he was somewhat frail, we knew there was every chance that the elderly actor would leave before the show was over. As we took our final bows, the girls and I squinted through the spotlights to see if we could make out anyone up there. We thought we spotted a blurred outline, and as soon as we got off stage it was confirmed that not only had Lord Olivier stayed throughout, but he'd loved the show and wanted to meet us for a chat if we had time to spare.

It's strange, but I can't recall ever being so excited at the prospect of meeting a famous person. It isn't that I'd been a great theatre-goer before or had followed his illustrious career particularly closely. It was just that here was some-one of such gigantic acting stature and experience that to my mind he had achieved a kind of legendary status. To be able to say I'd met and talked with Laurence Olivier would be a very special memory.

I wasn't disappointed. Immediately we got our make-up off, we rushed up to Dave Clark's *Time* suite, magnificently decked out in white silk like a potentate's palace, and for an hour discussed the show and theatre generally. He was fantastic, and for me personally very, very encouraging. I poured my heart out about the disappointment over our press treatment, and discovered that his opinion of pro-fessional theatre critics was about as low as mine. 'It's people who can't act who tend to write about acting,' he said.

That rang bells. I'll guarantee that the shrillest record and concert reviewers are themselves about as musical as a punctured bagpipe! Generally speaking, the people whose opinions mattered most were the ones who had paid for their tickets!

Strangely enough, I never could fathom out the attitude of other West End show companies towards us. Love it though I did, I came away from my year's foray into theatre with the impression that there's far more bitchiness in that department of show business than in our rock'n'roll world.

There's little to compare with the camaraderie that exists between singer and singer. No equivalent, for instance, of one star name being willing to do backing vocals for another. In the music world, it seems to me that there's a cohesion in the industry and we're mutually supportive in all sorts of ways. OK, there are individuals who naturally compete for sales and chart positions, but nevertheless there's a feeling of being part of an industry and being loyal to that.

In the West End, my experience was of being part of a company but nothing more. There seemed to be no broader family and, although there was a good deal of social exchange and visits to one another's matinées where possible, there was always a sense of 'us and them', 'our company against yours'.

It was as if one company felt threatened by another's success, although why that should be, when there were so many successful and established shows around – *Les Misérables*, *Cats*, *Chess*, *Phantom of the Opera*, *Starlight Express*, and so on – I can't imagine. Though, on second thoughts, perhaps it's to do with the relatively few jobs available at any one time, despite the success that the West End offers for dancers and singers. It's understandable that unemployment problems breed insecurities and jealousies, but I have to admit that I found those aspects of theatre probably the least appealing.

That's not to say I wouldn't jump at the chance of getting back. I still have this little intuition in my head about the potential of a play with music – not a musical in the familiar sense, but quite literally a play which is punctuated by about ten really great surefire hit rock songs. No recitative, that operatic-style sung dialogue. None of that repetitious stuff when a character speaks what someone has just sung. In my format, the songs would actually help forward the plot rather than merely embellishing or reinforcing it.

Just imagine the possibilities if the likes of Alan Tarney, Terry Britten (who now writes for Tina Turner) and John Farrar could be persuaded to collaborate on the song-writing, and someone like Derek Jacobi could be enlisted to give depth and credibility to the acting. It would take daring on the part of an actor like that, because the concept of a play with rock music isn't too familiar. And whereas the rock world is adventurous and continually forges ahead with new sounds and techniques, theatre is vastly more conservative. For the most part, any 'daring' at all seems concentrated on tilting at traditional morality – and long ago that became very dreary.

So, Derek, how about co-starring with this rock'n'roll upstart? Now on your part that would be daring 'for real'! And, for me, what a privilege!

2 TIME AND A HALF

2 TIME AND A HALF

I don't mind who knows it – I'm a dyed-in-the-wool, unashamed, square-eyed Trekkie. When it's 'Beam me up, Scottie' time on TV, the world outside as good as stops as Captain Kirk and his crew once more 'boldly go where no man has gone before'. So far I've videoed about forty of what I gather are the seventy-two *Star Trek* TV episodes, and, if the BBC stick with their reruns, I aim for a full house by the end of the century. Strange as it sounds, I'm still riveted – both by the plots and by the characters, despite watching some of the episodes over and over again.

The truth is it's not just *Star Trek*. I'm a sucker for science fiction full stop. The mere mention of bug-eyed monsters from space, or the hint of something nasty lurking in a rocket ship, and I'm hooked. Many's the time I've lined up at the cinema to see the latest sci-fi epic, desperately trying to look cool and nonchalant and to blend in with the rest of the punters, whose average age barely exceeds thirteen. It's at moments like that that I long for an instant face transplant! Even a false bushy beard would do, but I'd never summon up the nerve to wear it in case someone actually recognised me! As usual, I resort to the frequent-blowing-of-nose-into-large-handkerchief ploy – but there's a limit to how long you can blow! Being saddled with an easily recognised face is not always an advantage, I promise you.

My favourite full-length sci-fi move of all time is *Bladerunner*. For me it had depth and quality, and I was therefore totally flummoxed when one leading Christian magazine condemned it as insidious and harmful. Maybe I have too simple an approach to these things, and admittedly I'm not one for deep analysis or reading between the lines. Even so, my lasting impression of *Bladerunner* is of the dying android who drove a nail through his palm to keep himself alert enough to save a man's life. Not exactly accidental symbolism, I would have thought, and I for one appreciated it.

While undoubtedly it's the little boy in me that enjoys the adventure and excitement of science fiction, and while, like virtually all entertainment, sci-fi is high on escapism, there seems to be a dominant moral theme in many of these stories which often comes as welcome refreshment. I can't say I came out of *Star Trek IV*, for instance, like a caped crusader, but certainly I felt buoyed up because I was reminded very simply that good is better than evil. Now of course as a Christian I know that already, and moreover I know that the good-versus-evil issue has been settled once and for all by Jesus' death and resurrection. But in a world where we're bombarded so relentlessly with the devil's death-throes, so to speak – rape, terrorism, attacks on old people, child abuse, and goodness knows what else – it does me no harm at all to be caught up in a story where good is right and good triumphs. If you read this morning's newspaper, you could be excused for forming quite the reverse opinion.

Truth, they say, is stranger than fiction – certainly it's a good deal less palatable at times. Yet although there are obvious dangers involved in ducking out of the real world and escaping too often into make-believe and fantasy, the occasional visit can be positively beneficial. The all-crucial factor is that we keep the difference between the two in sharp focus.

Maybe with that bit of background you can understand why I was immediately 'grabbed' by the *Time* script. For years I'd dreamt of playing in a West End musical, and in fact whenever an interviewer asked me about any unful-filled ambitions that was the area I'd mention. Yet equally for years I'd been turning down scripts and ideas because they weren't sufficiently interesting. Either the storyline was poor or the music was duff, or it just wasn't my cup of tea. In most instances it was a combination of all three. Then along came Dave Clark with the manuscript of *Time*, and it was all there – competent commercial music (there's no way I could have done over four hundred performances of songs I didn't like!), an original idea, a strong moral storyline about human responsibility, and all that wrapped around with sci-fi imagination. Someone, I suspected, had been doing his homework.

On top of that, John Napier had been asked to design the set, and if anyone could make an outer-space story work on stage it was this brilliant guy, who'd already worked wonders with the sets of *Starlight Express*, *Cats* and *Les Misérables*.

Nevertheless, first time round, I declined the offer, simply because my diary was crammed for two or three years ahead and there was no way I could devote over a year to be more or less monopolised by one new project.

Happily for me Dave Clark was persistent and came back two years later and asked again, 'How about it?' Time was right (in both senses) and, for the first occasion ever in my career, we blocked out fifteen solid months to be in one place for one show.

And then came the doubts. The first time I read the script I loved it. The second time there was a niggle, and the more I read the more I realised that, as a Christian, there were certain lines in the story I just couldn't endorse. There was nothing immoral or suggestive, no bad language or violence – in fact quite the opposite, the whole thing was fantastically ethical.

What bugged me was that the truth according to *Time* didn't always square with the truth according to Scripture. Jesus, for instance, was referred to as a time lord; the Bible seemed to be quoted quite often, but not always accurately; and who was Akash? Was he really meant to be God in the likeness of Laurence Olivier? And what about that dogmatic statement that there was no such thing as death? Even apart from the Christian understanding, that was pretty daft, particularly for anyone who'd just lost a loved one.

So from the outset I had a dilemma. Here was a show that appealed professionally and which was morally good. The fact that the script was a cocktail of ideas from all sorts of philosophies and religions didn't bother me too greatly, as I learnt long ago that Christianity doesn't have an exclusive hold on all truth. You'll find strands of it wrapped up in all sorts of surprising packages, and what Dave Clark and his writers had done was to assemble many different strands and weave them together in a kind of outer-space courtroom drama.

On trial was the human race, for greedily exploiting and deliberately destroying its planet. Whole species of animals were threatened with extinction because of man's self-interest. Scientific achievement was being directed to destructive ends. And injustice and oppression meant that millions were starving while others grew fat. Inevitably the verdict of the judges was a unanimous 'Guilty', and earth and all its inhabitants were doomed to dispersal. Only the pleading and promises of a reluctant earth representative finally merited at least a temporary reprieve.

That was the gist of the plot, and it was that which was written off as shallow and of little consequence by several media critics. I couldn't understand their reaction then, and I don't now. Maybe their disdain simply reflected their own personal values – or rather the lack of them. But back to my dilemma.

Could a show which encouraged us to be more concerned for the earth and for each other be wrong about Christian truth? Or, more accurately, was it likely to misrepresent Christian truth and be a false teacher? There are plenty of weird sects and so-called 'men of God' around, and people are confused enough as it is with so many varying opinions and interpretations. The last thing I wanted for *Time* was to add yet more.

I must confess it didn't help any when a couple of my closest Christian friends came back with negative reactions after reading the script. 'Morally fine, but theologically up the spout,' was their opinion. 'Just be prepared for a lot of flak from the church,' warned one. In fact there was none, but I'll come to that in a minute.

What I had to come to terms with was that this wasn't a Christian show as such. For sure, there was a lot in it that Christians would believe, but essentially it was science fiction, definitely not science fact, as Dave Clark preferred to call it. At least for the time being, galactic courtrooms belong fairly and squarely to the realm of fiction, and that was my starting-point. Consequently, when I read numerous references to God and Jesus, I fixed an early meeting to determine script amendments. Much as I love science fiction, there's no way I was going to let Jesus become a kind of glorified Captain Kirk. In my book he's the unique and eternal Son of God, and to put him on a par with some 'heavy' time lord – however impressive as a stage character – would be pretty demeaning, to say the least.

Although in part it was a battle, all credit to Dave Clark for listening and agreeing to most of my requests. Certain lines were cut altogether, blatant references to God and

Jesus were changed or deleted, and the 'time lord' descrip-
tion became 'a guiding light' – hardly adequate, but I could
live with that.

No longer did I feel that *Time* was riding on a pseudo-
Christian bandwagon. And in a way it was its deficiency
that convinced me the show's message was not misleading
and that I would not be compromising my Christian stand
by playing in it. No one, it seemed to me, could be steered
by *Time* into any false or harmful doctrines, simply because
it made no attempt to offer constructive solutions to man's
problems. Its analysis was true enough – man was greedy
and selfish, he should be more caring and responsible, but
how? That was the crunch question, and *Time* offered no
answer.

In a way it was personally a bit frustrating, and part of me
would have loved an evangelist to come on stage at the end
of each show and qualify and complete all that had been
said and sung. As it was, I had to be content with my
'Jesus – One Way' sign after taking applause at the end.
Although I couldn't verbalise it, it was my means of indicating that there is only one way to deal with the evil or sin
that's in us, and that's through Jesus.

What the audience didn't know was that every night,
when the godlike figure of Akash told us there was no such
thing as death and that love was everlasting and that we'd
live for ever, I'd look up at the benign face of Laurence
Olivier and say to myself, 'Yes, but there's no death only
because Jesus died and offers us eternity; it isn't automatic.
And, yes, love is everlasting, but only because Christ has
shown us how to live and does his loving through us.
And, yes, we do live for ever, but only if we accept him.'
What Akash was saying wasn't actually wrong, and for
Christians in the audience it was totally true, but for every-
one else it was all the stuff of appealing pipedreams.

It was the same with that finale song of mine. In a sense,
it *is* potentially 'in every one of us to be wise', but the lyric
didn't go on to explain how. The Bible's solution is that, 'If
any of you lacks wisdom, he should ask God . . . and it will
be given to him.' Now I knew that, and so did thousands of
Christians who heard the song, but for many others it
merely raised more question marks.

Left to our own devices, humanity is anything but wise –
clever, intelligent even, but certainly short on wisdom, as

history demonstrates over and over again. If only humanity really could pull itself up by its own bootstraps, if only it were possible to screw up every ounce of will-power on New Year's Eve and keep those fine resolutions intact right through the year. Humanistic philosophy suggests we should struggle to do just that, but in my book it's simply a recipe for frustration. This little human, for one, doesn't have the ability. I've tried, but it doesn't work. I know what I'd like to be, I know how I'd like to live, but try as I might, somehow I miss the mark by miles.

Paul the apostle experienced the same thing: 'I have the desire to do what is good,' he wrote, 'but I cannot carry it out. For what I do is not the good I want to do; no, the evil I do not want to do – this I keep on doing.' That, I'm sure, is a common experience for all of us, at least when we're being honest.

Time, then, graphically spelt out the world's shortcomings, went on to dangle all those wonderful carrots about living in harmony and being loving and caring and wise, but, for me at least, failed to offer the all-important key. It was the truth, but not all the truth; it was part of the truth, but not the whole truth. Again, it was like Paul writing, 'I can do everything' and forgetting to add the critical qualifying phrase '. . . through him [Christ] who gives me strength'.

So, yes, I did go into the show with just a slight uneasiness, even though Dave had accepted most of the script changes I wanted. But what I believed, and what I discovered once again, was that if you offer something to God and ask him to use it he does just that. I've done it with my career scores of times.

Very simply I say to God, 'Here is my art form; I'll perform it to the best of my ability, I'll try not to bring dishonour to you; please use it and let any glory that's going be for yourself.' I record a song, even a track like 'Devil Woman', for instance, with no apparent Christian message, and offer it to the Lord and let him do the rest. I heard of two people, would you believe, who became Christians as an indirect result of listening to that particular song. And 'We Don't Talk Any More' was another example. One girl understood the lyric in the context of prayer, and it was all the prompting she needed to restore her relationship with God.

We weren't long into *Time* before I knew that God had his seal on that too. Letters started to arrive, explaining how the story had been a challenge to rethink old values. Instead of leading up blind alleys, its very lack of solution was prompting people to pursue answers for themselves.

Instead of flak from the church, as my friend predicted, I was delighted when one Christian youth magazine urged its readers to see the show and posed a whole set of questions as discussion-starters based on the plot. That seemed to set the pattern. Instead of carping criticism, which I half-expected, there was a constructive approach which proved a tremendous personal encouragement. Churches organised coach parties to the show and Sunday sermons were preached on its theme.

One clergyman on the staff of London's vibrant All Souls' Church reckoned it was invaluable pre-evangelism and, although I initially thought that might be going a little over the top, he was proved absolutely right. My office has a batch of letters from people who saw the show over the course of the year, were moved by what they heard, and miraculously made the step from *Time* to the gospel.

Towards the end of the run, perhaps the greatest thrill of all was to hear from a clergyman friend up north with the news that a well-known showbiz celebrity had been jolted to think so much about his own life and attitude that he'd made a commitment to Christ as a result. Unbeknown to me, this guy had slipped into the show about six times; he'd never come backstage and never made himself known to the front-of-house management. Presumably he was too wrapped up working through the personal implications and listening to that 'still small voice'. A few weeks later I got a letter from him, confirming what he'd done and thanking me for the show. I now look forward to meeting him and finding out just what it was that communicated so profoundly.

Soon after I finished at the Dominion, someone remarked what a pity it was that I'd had to cut out most of my Christian ministry for over a year. By that he meant no more visiting churches and universities around the country to talk and to answer questions about my faith. I realised what he meant, but personally I think it was a misunderstanding and far too narrow a view of Christian ministry.

As I see it, the Christian's life is his or her ministry. Public speaking is just one relatively small facet of it, that some Christians feel inclined to do and others don't. A Christian greengrocer has a ministry, and that's the way he runs his shop and how he deals with his customers. The Christian teacher's ministry is at school and revolves around the excellence of his or her teaching and relationships with pupils and staff. When a Christian retires and draws a pension, Christian ministry doesn't take a back seat all of a sudden. It may follow new avenues; possibly quieter, less active ones, but definitely no less important. The mistake we make is thinking that God is concerned about large numbers and big events and that, unless we're taking part in at least three meetings a week, we're somehow backsliding.

The fact is that, during all the preparations for and the actual performance of *Time*, I probably took part in only three or four public meetings, but then that wasn't my priority ministry for that particular period. 'Ministry' for me was just being in *Time*, not to hand out tracts to fellow artists or to do other things 'on the side', but to be committed to the show and, through my attitude and behaviour and professional performance, to be Christ's representative in that theatre. And, believe me, that's no second-class ministry.

Just as the Christian office worker has a unique role because no one else is doing exactly the same job or contacting exactly the same people, so my responsibility in the show was unique. First and foremost I was on that stage, night after night, not simply as an actor and a singer, but as a Christian actor and singer, and that had to make a difference. If I gave a shabby performance or was rowing with other members of the cast, it was the Lord I was letting down, and that's the one thing I'd determined should never happen.

So for me *Time* was a matter of Cliff the Christian presenting a facet of truth about the world's problems to approaching three-quarters of a million people. I'll never know just how many of them were provoked into some sort of useful and positive response because of it, or may even have found it a stepping-stone to eventual Christian commitment. As I say, I certainly heard of one who did.

Whether or not the *Time* experience helped me to grow personally as a Christian is another issue. I've little doubt

Jeff Shankley, TIME's awesome Melchisedic, was fabulous to act with, and I always relished our nightly courtroom exchanges. *(Photo: Hanne Jordan)*

Right: Seven and sometimes eight TIME performances a week for a whole year was tough, but I never missed one – not even for a holiday.
(Photo: Theresa Wassif)

Below: For a year I shared the TIME stage with the 15-foot tall, disembodied head of Lord Olivier. The holographic effect was extraordinary and theatrically unique.
(Photo: Theresa Wassif)

(Photo: Theresa Wassif)

Which one's Cliff?

Below: How could anyone not be moved? Charity may start at home, but it certainly doesn't end there.

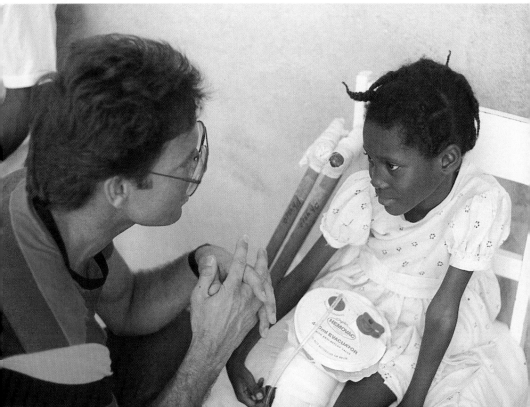

George Hoffman, Tear Fund's General Director, (left) gets the low-down on one of Haiti's problems from its man on the spot. Invariably I come back from these trips not so much depressed by the needs, but bowled over by the commitment and compassion shown by the men and women who've volunteered to live and work there.

I reckon a penny for every autograph I've signed would pay off a few national debts! I can't pretend I enjoy the occupational chore but most times I grin and bear it. *(Photo: Hanne Jordan)*

You'd be clapped out too, I promise, after an hour's run-around on court with Sue Barker.

The high and the not-so-mighty!

After discovering that Steffi Graf was in the audience at one of my German concerts, it took less than 24 hours to set up 'a hit' with her and her coach, Pavil Slozil.

Ronnie Corbett and Peter Cook aren't in quite the same class, but they brought the house down at my annual Pro-Celebrity Tennis Tournament at Brighton.   *(Photo: John McGoran)*

Court napping. *(Photo: Colin Ramsay)*

that the whole process of figuring out in the first instance all the potential theological pitfalls, amending this and deleting that, was a valuable experience. Similarly, to think through and to decide how to make the Chris Wilder role plausible and believable was a new type of challenge, and I found it both demanding and helpful.

What was decidedly unhelpful was the problem I had with attending church. The fact is that I just didn't! Perhaps I didn't realise how much seven or eight performances a week would take out of me, but when Sundays came round I felt I needed to stay in bed all day, and when I did eventually get up I didn't want to go anywhere, least of all to a public place, and that included church. (Strangely enough, it felt as though every Sunday I was on the verge of flu, although that must have been more psychological than physical.) Even with hindsight, I still don't know the answer to that problem. I know I should have gone, I know it would have done me good spiritually, but for six days of the week I put in a lot of effort – physically, mentally and emotionally – and on Sundays I was drained. I can appreciate now what a tension that must mean for the Christian actor who's regularly in the West End or in rep. The first thing to suffer is your Sundays, and, believe me, they do become precious.

Forgive a little soul-baring, but even at the best of times I don't find church-going easy. I can never stop being Cliff Richard, so whatever church I go to, however well-meaning the members are, there will always be some who've seen me on *Top of the Pops* or whatever, and in their eyes I'm a celebrity, a star, a famous person who, like a chimp in a zoo, is there for the public gaze at all times and in all situations. Now for me that's so much boloney, but I understand that that's the nature of the fame game.

There's just nothing I dislike more than being trapped against a pillar after a service and having to autograph dozens of Bibles and bits of paper. It hardly seems in the spirit of things to escape through a side door immediately the last hymn's over, but that's what I do if it's practically possible. So, with that pressure always there at the best of times, you can imagine how I felt on those 'clapped-out' Sundays in 1986 and 1987. But, so long as the Lord understands, which he does, that's all that matters, and the last thing he intended the Sabbath to be was a legal drag!

But having said that, don't go jumping to any conclusions that church isn't important. It is, and by now I'm back to my erratic kind of church life. Like everyone else, I need the fellowship of other Christians, as well as the opportunity to enjoy God with them, and I well remember the old illustration of what happens to a lump of coal when it drops from the fire on to the hearth. Gradually it loses its glow, becomes cold, and generates nothing. That's why, as a rule, I'll get to some Sunday service, even on an overseas tour.

But back to the *Time* situation. It was great – and not, I believe, a mere coincidence – that I was 'looked after' in two ways which compensated just a bit for missing church.

If you'd passed by the Dominion dressing-room on at least half a dozen occasions during the run, you'd have heard some pretty unlikely music wafting through the corridor. I doubt if backstage Dominion has been host to Bible studies and praise meetings too often in the past, but they certainly took place while I was there.

You'd be surprised to learn just how many Christians there are working in professional theatre these days, and a group associated with the Arts Centre Group make it a priority to visit different theatres in the West End where Christians are 'in residence' and encourage and support them with their prayers, and share an hour of worship. I loved it, and it gave me a valuable chance to invite a few others from the cast and crew to join us.

It was fabulous, for instance, to hear that the girl who fixed my microphones each night was a 'baby Christian' herself and to share her excitement when her boyfriend, also from the backstage crew, made a commitment too.

I've already told you how the cast and I became really close as the year went by. We made a point of eating out regularly together after the show, and inevitably I got the usual pummelling about what I believe and why. For me that's no hardship, and many's the night we'd emerge from a restaurant at around 3 a.m., with minds still very much awake.

Probably the best discussions of all were at the Arts Centre Group HQ, near Waterloo, and I felt it was tremendous that actors and actresses, not only from *Time* but also from other major West End musicals, were interested enough to spend hours after a show talking about

God and Jesus. Maybe those of us who earn our living in a make-believe theatrical world need to know about truth and reality more than most.

The second of those little compensations came in the form of a book. A couple of Christian friends who work for a First Division football team – you do find Christians in the most improbable places these days! – came to the show and gave me a volume entitled *The One Year Bible*. Now I'd never systematically worked through the whole Bible before, and that sparked off twelve months of some of my most avid reading. Call it coincidence, if you like, but for me it was as though God was saying, 'OK, church is tricky for a while, but no excuses about Bible study!' Get out of that!

Unquestionably *Time* had its shortcomings. It didn't claim to be a great literary work. Nor, for me at least, was it a Christian show in the sense that it set out to present any balanced biblical truth. Yet from the moment I made that first initial commitment to it, I dared to believe that God could do something with it – and, despite us all, I believe he did.

The show's title inevitably produced endless puns. I lost track of how many people referred to me 'doing time'. The funny thing was that they all thought they were the first to think of it. It's amazing how many times – there it is again – the word crops up in ordinary conversation, and I think I'll be stuck with its special connotations for the rest of my days.

'Beyond Time' seemed a perfect title for my gospel concert tour which followed about eight weeks after that tearful last night and after a couple of desperately needed holidays in the Caribbean and in Portugal. 'Beyond Time's' dual meaning needed no explanation, and it was a great opportunity to capitalise on *Time*'s theme and to dot all the i's and cross the t's. 'OK, *Time* had a great story to tell,' I was able to say, 'but here's an even better one – and it comes with genuine authority.' What I couldn't verbalise in *Time*, I made up for beyond, and we were able to pass nearly £100,000 to *Tear Fund* and other charities into the bargain. A useful three weeks!

3 MUSIC TO THE EARS

3 MUSIC TO THE EARS

I have a theory that, in a few thousand years' time, our ears will have evolved into black spongy blobs and we'll probably all be stone deaf. The first mutants have already arrived. You see them, apparently in a world of their own, in restaurants, trains, even walking along crowded pavements. They all have the same glazed eyes and faraway expressions. Ears once exposed to the elements are plugged with small metallic implants, the tell-tale mark of the Walkman headset!

I dare say I'd have been first in the queue if the technology had been around in the Fifties. To escape totally into a world of Elvis music would have been my idea of heaven. As it was, the gramophone received a relentless pounding, and neighbours on our Cheshunt council estate moved in and out in rapid succession.

Today it's different. Call it age if you like (I prefer to think of it as maturity), but I no longer feel the need to be bathed in music – Elvis or anyone else – for sixteen hours a day. Apart from on holiday, where I admit to adopting antisocial habits and clamp the old headphones on for hours at a time while the sun cooks me, it's only in the car that I do any serious listening. Although I invariably drive with the windows fully wound up, rumour has it that my car stereo is the equivalent of a three-mile early warning system. I confess it's loud. Startled motorists have been known to drive up kerbs as they're overtaken by what they assume to be a portable fairground.

To satisfy the curiosity of any hi-fi buffs, I've had six speakers fitted to the car's rear ledge; two of them are big bass woofers, two just take the middle range, and the other two are tweeters for the top. At the front there are four more speakers, so, with graphic equalisers, you can actually pick out and accentuate the bass, mids or tops – whatever area of sound you want to listen for specifically. With that little lot in the confines of a VW Golf, who needs wall-to-wall amplifiers!

In case, by the way, any traffic cops are making mental notes to check me out for reckless driving, I'd better add that there's no way I'm blasting out decibels every mile I travel. Frankly, I get fed up with listening to a permanent barrage of music, and I'm just as likely to be under the influence of a Radio 4 chat show played at a very modest volume! Besides which, it's a fallacy to think that loud music saps all your concentration. To my mind, good pop music doesn't demand concentration. If it does, then it really isn't working. I need a song to appeal within the first fifteen seconds, so if you have to play a track over and over again to find something good, the chances are there's nothing good to find.

For me, the car is the greatest place to listen – no distractions, no telephone calls, no visitors. On a familiar route your brain goes into automatic cruising, and the music just flows, but I guarantee I'd be alert enough for the quickest of emergency stops if the need arose. Honestly, m'lud!

Let me preface some thoughts about music by stating the obvious. Musical tastes are totally subjective. Just as I can't force my musical opinion on anyone else, so no one can tell me what I should or shouldn't enjoy. I know what appeals to me, therefore, whereas my need for 'immediacy' in a song may sound superficial to some, to my ear it's a vital part of a song's construction. I need music to entertain. If it can convey a message as well, then that's a bonus, but it isn't necessary. It's the music that has to appeal. And, for a reason that I can't explain, neither jazz nor classical forms appeal one little bit.

I can admire the vocal techniques of singers like Peggy Lee and Morgana King, and I appreciate the tone and quality of their voices, but that's as far as it goes. The music itself does nothing for me, even though I recognise that elements of it are good and certainly clever. Similarly with classical music. I can appreciate the brilliance of the musicianship and the complexity of a score, and I'd never dream of 'putting it down' as such, yet for me it can stay in its concert halls. André Previn may reckon that classical is the greatest musical art form. I'm adamant that it's rock 'n' roll. Thank goodness there's both of us!

When I look back over twenty-five years or more, I'm surprised at how consistent my musical tastes have been. Certainly I'm much more discerning now in what I choose to play. Long gone are the days when I'd go out and buy just about everything released on the pop market. When I was a kid it was theoretically possible to do that because, compared to today, there was so little product. But, as I got into making music myself, I became less interested in playing other people's music merely for the sake of it, and now in fact a fair chunk of what I listen to is professionally compulsory. It enables me to keep up with what's going on. Yet, when I do find an album or a single that I really enjoy – and a combination of melody and aggressive backing track is the perfect formula – I tend to play it to death.

After all these years, 'flavours of the month' in the music industry don't influence me one bit. Conversely, if the so-called trendy experts think it's old hat to play Lionel Richie, for instance, then to heck with them – I love him.

If you assume, though, that the arrival of a few grey hairs marks an inevitable transition in taste from raunchy rock to mellow MOR, you'd be wrong. For a start I wouldn't have put all the gear in the car to play Val Doonican at maximum decibels! But ZZ Top – that's another matter. For me there's nothing to beat heavy bass and drums, and when I'm eighty I can't imagine I'll have any other preference. Just imagine – a generation of geriatric rockers – we're on our way, folks!

Unlike Mike Read, who's a walking encyclopaedia of the pop industry, I don't rate myself as any kind of expert as far as facts and figures are concerned. When I went on Mike's *Pop Quiz* on TV I was terrified I wouldn't know a thing, although as it turned out I didn't do that badly. There was a period in my life when I could have named everyone who ever played on an Elvis or Ricky Nelson record. James Burton, D. J. Fontana, Bill Black and Scotty Moore were all legendary characters and fantastic musicians. But today it's different. Musical standards generally have improved so incredibly that I might hear a brilliant guitar solo on a record and not even bother to check out who it was. There are just so many guys who can do it now that it's hard to get excited over any one individual.

The late Fifties and early Sixties were pioneering days in music. There was only one Scotty Moore, only one James

Burton. These days there are almost as many fabulous guitarists, bass players and drummers about as there are record releases. What is perhaps endangered is spontaneity. Technical advances have made it possible to record mind-blowing sounds and effects. On stage, for instance, we use three keyboards which, once patched up, give us the equivalent of the London Symphony Orchestra without the cost! Although the synthetic sound isn't an exact copy of, say, a violin, there are instances when I actually prefer the copy. Sometimes the pure violin, beautiful though it is, doesn't suit a particular song as well as a synth sound which, even though based on a violin expression, is just that little bit wider, thinner, bigger, or whatever. Nowadays it's fantastic to have the freedom to search for a sound that's tailor-made to suit one particular musical phrase, and synthesizer technology has opened up a whole new dimension of creativity.

But before the Musicians' Union goes up the wall and puts my membership card through the shredder, let me add that, although the synthesizer most definitely is here to stay and will inevitably develop even more amazing output, there's no way that machines can ever take over entirely from the flesh-and-blood musician. My synth sounds only work when they're played alongside a real bass, real guitar and real drum kit. A discerning mix of the two is terrific. Overdosing on the synthetic can produce clever music, but it's likely to be clinical and heartless. A drum machine is a godsend for the young musician struggling to produce top-quality demos, but for finished product give me the panic of the berserk drummer any day. For, sure, a drum machine guarantees a rock-solid tempo with no risk of variation, while within a three-minute piece of music even the best of drummers will tilt just a fraction or find it impossible to maintain exactly the same 'feel' from beginning to end. But that's the essence of music, and no drum machine, however wonderful, can compete with the drummer who does his fill, follows his instinct, and gets it right.

Everyone who's ever worked with me in a recording studio knows I'm a stickler for singing in tune. But, while I insist on repairing any duff notes and getting everything right as far as the ear can tell, I know full well it's impossible to achieve absolute musical perfection – whatever that is.

It's mind-boggling to me, for instance, when I'm assured that, if a piano could be tuned to perfection it would sound diabolical when played along with other normally tuned instruments. To the musically educated there's probably a simple answer to that, and I'm sure I'll learn, but it seems evident, on the strength of that alone, that technically flawless music is neither desirable nor practically possible, at least not so far as we 'live' singers and musicians are concerned. But then we're only human – well, most of us!

However, musical excellence isn't a problem. What is, dare I say, is the dearth of really great songs. In my opinion it isn't enough just to make good sounds. Studio technique is so far advanced these days that any band's first-off record can sound wonderful if they know what they're doing. But the crunch for me is the song, and so often I buy an album on the strength of a really appealing single, only to find that six or seven tracks are little more than instantly forgettable fillers. Good sounds maybe, but certainly not great songs. And, for my money, if there are only three decent songs on an album, I'd rather buy three separate choice singles, than have to plough through half an hour of rubbish.

Incidentally, I do like singers actually to be able to sing. Many of those I hear on *Top of the Pops* and the like really can't, and get away with a noise that's not even distinctive. One thing I do pride myself on is that, whether or not people like my voice, they won't be hearing any bum notes, and that's more than I can say for a number of today's performers.

But back to songs and, as someone who's put out goodness knows how many albums over the years – I think the current total is around fifty, of which twenty-seven have Top Ten charted – I know only too well how hard it is to maintain standards. (Incidentally, I hear that those twenty-seven albums have equalled Frank Sinatra's UK tally. Only Elvis to overtake!) Record companies, keen to exploit the market, put the squeeze on for an album by such-and-such a date, and the artist is forced to compromise by recording material that isn't up to scratch. Occasionally there's the welcome exception who sustains fantastic song quality throughout. Lionel Richie's *Can't Stop Now* album and Michael Jackson's *Thriller* stick in my mind, and Fleetwood Mac too seem to manage amazing consistency.

Of my own albums I rate *Always Guaranteed*, *I'm No Hero* and *Wired For Sound* as probably featuring the best selections of songs. Alan Tarney material such as 'Some People', 'Dreaming', 'A Heart Will Break Tonight', 'A Little In Love', 'Take Another Look' and 'Everyman' were just class songs, and I consider myself fortunate in being offered them. As a rule I don't record any songs which I don't actually like, but there's a world of difference between 'likeable' and 'sheer class'. Sometimes you have to settle for the first, hoping of course that your fans will share your taste. It's a reasonable assumption that they will, or presumably they wouldn't be fans in the first place!

It isn't that there's any lack of budding songwriters. Hardly a day goes by without a bundle of cassettes arriving either at home or at the office. There's no way I can listen to all of them personally, but they're heard at the office, and anything promising gets passed back. Ninety-nine times out of a hundred, I'm afraid, they get rejected – but not because there's anything intrinsically wrong with them. Some songs are pleasant enough, and most are excellent demos, but the plain fact is that they just don't make the hairs on my neck stand on end – and that's the test. 'Miss You Nights', 'Devil Woman', 'We Don't Talk Any More', 'Please Don't Tease' and 'Move It' are all totally different from each other, yet all of them are songs that gave me goose-bumps on first hearing. I can't explain why, and I can't analyse the ingredient that created the magic effect. Maybe it's simply down to 'body chemistry', but when hungry writers ask me what I look for in a song, the only help I can give is to say that it has to pass the 'hair on the neck' and 'goose-bump' test. Hardly profound wisdom, and pretty useless advice, but it's all I know.

Music has to be emotive. It needs to cause anger, sadness, romance or just plain happiness, and some writers don't have that knack. Although it's hard to separate lyric from melody, the structure of a song is far more important to me as a singer than even the finest message-laden lyric, and many's the time I've 'passed' on a worthwhile lyric because the music is either easily predictable or instantly forgettable.

That's particularly true in the realm of Christian music. I mustn't be too cynical, but I get dozens of tapes from no doubt well-meaning and sincere Christian people who tell me that the Lord has 'given' them a song which they feel I should record. My only conclusion is that the Lord must have a pretty unmusical ear, because much of it isn't, shall we say, that good!

To be fair, I ought to underline again that musical taste is highly subjective and, because I don't earn my living singing gospel music, I can hardly claim to be a gospel singer. But, as a commercial 'pop rocker', I have to apply the same criteria to Christian music as I would to regular 'secular' material, and at grass roots, in this country at least, it doesn't always compare too well.

Having said that, there are a growing number of Christian writers who are beginning to make their mark, and it's only a matter of time, I feel, before hard-nosed DJs and radio station and record company executives will be forced to bury their prejudices and be as open to promoting Christian lyrics as they are to just about every other kind of 'message'. And by a Christian lyric I don't necessarily mean inspirational or worship material. That has its place – and it's in church rather than in the charts. Don't expect 'Hallelujah, praise the Lord' to impress a company A & R man. Why should it – unless he's a Christian, and there aren't too many of those around! But a fresh slant on a street-level issue will be judged by no other criterion than its commerciality. That means it must entertain as well as communicate, and that's no easy combination. It's taken the gospel music industry a long time to come to terms with the fact that entertainment isn't actually a dirty word or a worldly compromise.

Not so long ago I took part for the first time in a huge American gospel festival and, although the atmosphere was fantastic and the music was of an incredibly high quality, I couldn't help feeling there were still enormous inhibitions on the part of artists to actually *perform* their material. One relatively successful Christian singer after another came on stage and, although it would be hard to fault what was said or sung, there was a distinct lack of creative or imaginative presentation, and that's where I feel that a few of us on this side of the Atlantic have something to offer.

It's why Sheila Walsh, for instance, whom I introduced on my gospel concerts in the UK, has made such an impression in the States. She isn't trapped into any clichéd gospel concert formula and isn't afraid to tell audiences what they *need* to hear rather than what they *want* to hear. Her performance has upset a few conservative die-hards because she dares to use the art form that stage presentation demands. Rock 'n' roll has colossal resources of strength and drama, and Sheila is one of the few Christian artists I've seen who tries to harness it. Impressive lighting and thoughtful performance shouldn't detract from the Christian content. If it does, it's being wrongly used. In skilful hands it enhances and underlines lyrical content and personal testimony.

Think of the lighting I use for 'Miss You Nights', for instance. The whole object of the lighting plot is to help people focus on the lyric. Pyrotechnics would be ludicrous for a beautiful love song, so we wash the stage with warm light and, by bouncing laser beams off a mirrorball, we create those 'midnight diamonds' of the lyric. What the audience sees connects with what they hear, and the overall effect is more vivid and lasting.

This is all the more important, then, when we have something really great to say. If we can convey our gospel message through the eyes of an audience, as well as through their ears, then hopefully they will have double the chance of remembering!

The Christian scene is of course still struggling with the legacy of a puritanical and prejudiced past that believes the stage is owned and controlled – lock, stock and barrel – by the devil. Although Christians have made some pretty convincing assaults on his territory, a few weird hang-ups do little to help the cause of artistic progress. Would you believe that, in some parts of the US market, it's frowned upon to use any red stage lighting? Red, it's claimed, is 'the devil's own colour' and its effect is 'sinister and evil, and to be avoided at all costs'. Some otherwise reasonable Christians sincerely believe that, and, although it's an extreme example, it illustrates the kind of negative and discouraging attitude that 'puts the mockers on' creativity.

A more common justification for mediocre presentation is simply that complex rigs and effects machines cost too much. To an extent that's true, of course. Hiring and trucking and operating today's sophisticated stage technology can certainly involve mega-bucks, but that's where ingenuity comes in. Effective presentation and creative performance need not cost a fortune, and my plea is not for lavish over-the-top spending, but for more thought and care to be given to maximising what there is. Half a dozen lamps, if cleverly used, can be more effective than a complex rig with lights flashing at random merely for the sake of it.

I'm a little reluctant to raise the spectre of the old pop gospel controversy, because hopefully it may have died a discreet death. At least for the present it appears reasonably comatose. The debate centred on whether rock 'n' roll was a legitimate musical form for Christian lyrics. The relatively small number of Christians who maintained the two were incompatible based their case on the belief that the rock 'n' roll structure was essentially of the devil. There was therefore no way that a Christian singer could use it as a form of communication, although presumably other musical styles – classical, jazz, MOR, country and western, and so on – were permissible.

From the outset I've had little time or patience for this argument, although I maintain respect for the integrity of some of its spokesmen. Try as I might, I find no reason, logic or wisdom in those who would encourage young Christians to burn their rock albums. Like most way-out and extreme attitudes, the Bonfire Brigade originated in the USA, although happily it's never reached such hysterical lengths here. Of course let's teach Christians who are young in the faith to discern between what is God-honouring and what isn't, and there's no way I'd defend all the trash that's put out under the banner of rock 'n' roll. But discernment is the name of the game, not groundless sweeping prejudice. Believe me, there's plenty of country and western that's based on very dubious morality. And, from what I hear tell, the habits of some of those classical composers would make your hair curl!

My plea is not to raise negative, slightly ludicrous voices, and tell our kids not to listen. You may as well tell them to avoid TV and the cinema. All these art forms, whether we like it or not, are a part of our culture. They're popular, and potentially they're a colossal influence. The challenge for the Christian punter is to listen and then to choose. The necessity for the Christian communicator and artist is to move into those media and to ensure that choice actually exists.

Sadly, whenever a Christian pressure group – or anyone else, come to that – picks up the cudgels to campaign for a cause, there always seems to be a loony fringe ready to jump on the bandwagon and torpedo credibility. Have you come across the back-masking fanatics? Back-masking is the term for what, to me, is the totally pointless exercise of recording a message on vinyl that is only decipherable when played backwards. Don't ask me how you do it, or how you actually play the album backwards, it's beyond me. But apparently some bands, heavy metal groups in particular, I gather, have spent time, engineering skill and presumably money achieving just that. The messages were usually obscene and sometimes allegedly satanic.

Now I've no way of telling how widespread the practice has been, and I suspect that no one else genuinely knows. But for the Christians without a cause it offered a field day. Here was real tangible ammunition to prove that the whole rock 'n' roll scene was through-and-through corrupt, evil and devilish. So what happened? I received a letter from a concerned friend in Australia, telling me about a Christian group over there who were circulating a hit list of artists who had indulged in 'subtle indoctrination' through back-masking. Sure enough, I was on it. And the track, of all tracks, that was supposed to contain some foul message when reversed was 'When I Survey The Wondrous Cross'. I honestly didn't know whether to laugh or cry. Can you imagine what sort of mind it is that actually goes to the lengths of reversing a track and then construing some intelligible meaning from the gobbledegook that results. Perhaps a few artists have toyed with subversive messages. More fool them, because I can't believe many people heard them – apart, of course, from silly little misguided people in Australia and elsewhere who need their knuckles smacked and a major reassessment of their Christian priorities.

Unfortunately, for most people the phrase 'gospel music' still means hymns, George Beverley Shea, and negro spirituals. And without the media's cooperation it's hard to prove otherwise. In fact Christian songs can and should be as gutsy, professional and entertaining as anything else in today's hit charts, and to get away from that unhelpful 'gospel' tag, I coined the phrase 'rockspel' music to describe just that – Christian pop rock. Time will tell whether it catches on.

Those who've seen me in concert will know that I love the challenge of a stage performance. For me concerts should be just as much theatre as legitimate drama, and I could no more go on stage and do a static set, with hands stuck in pockets, than sing rock 'n' roll after a five-course meal. As I've said, virtually anyone these days can go in a studio and make a record. It may not sell, but it can be a passable enough effort. But on stage, in front of a crowd, there's no hiding place. And the challenge is not only to give a song a visual dimension, but to reproduce the same sound live that perhaps you spent weeks achieving in the studio. Sometimes after a concert people say that what they heard was 'just like the record'. I find that probably the most satisfying praise of all.

If you've got the impression that I've a soft spot for my industry, you'd be absolutely right. In fact I'm unreservedly committed to it. I realise full well that it's given me far more than any other could possibly have done. However, having established that, there are aspects of the business which disturb me, and I hope I'll be forgiven for a gripe or two. At least it's not sour grapes, and criticism comes best from within the family!

Basically, I wish our industry would wake up to its responsibilities to the kids who buy the records. For the most part, record companies seem to adopt an attitude of 'anything goes so long as it sells', and it's high time there were a few self-imposed restraints and disciplines. Take merchandising, for instance. Although, in fairness, it's not the record companies themselves that sell record paraphernalia, but quite independent companies who ride off the back of music trends and fashions.

It's perfectly legitimate to sell T-shirts, photographs, badges and what-have-you at concerts – they do it at mine – but why so often at rip-off prices? There seldom appears to be any effective quality control, and heavy-duty selling to virtually captive and very young audiences strikes me as all wrong. Even if Dad goes along for the ride, he's bludgeoned into parting with cash he probably can't afford for a cheap Jack T-shirt for his thirteen-year-old daughter, simply because it's hard to say no.

In a way, I suppose, you can't blame the merchandisers for selling, as, in most instances, it's up to parents to teach their kids to be sensible with money. Hard though it is, I have a feeling that Dad should say 'No' more often!

More serious is the overall 'message' that the industry conveys to impressionable kids. I don't want to sound like a latter-day Mary Whitehouse, even though I have great respect for the lady and think she's right nine times out of ten, but the plain fact is that the pop industry does wield colossal influence in the lives of children from really young ages (I know four-year-olds who can recite 'Living Doll' by heart), and I'd love to see some sign that they at least acknowledge it. Ideally it would be great if the artists managed to get their public lives sufficiently together to be at least a neutral example rather than a destructive one. But sadly our business doesn't allow its new 'stars' to be real people. Hype and image are the name of the game, and often artists make the fatal mistake of believing their own hand-outs.

I know from personal experience how difficult it is when you're only eighteen to handle the sudden influx of money or to be hounded relentlessly by the media. Somehow in my day it wasn't fraught with quite so many dangers, and there were only a handful of us who actually acquired pop 'stardom', whereas today there are many. And I have to say, from the safety of middle age, that when you're seventeen or eighteen you're still trying to find your feet as an adult and it takes something of a superman or woman in that pressurised pop cauldron to cope with the incredible amount of experiences that are part of the new lifestyle. Believe me, it's hard to control your own desires and feelings in those circumstances, and no wonder we read time and again of singers and musicians who seem publicly to be fantastically successful, only to have their private lives become pathetic shambles. The same would be true in any walk of life where wealth was accumulated very quickly, but maybe in other professions there are more checks, more answerability.

The recording star is a law unto himself, and that's where I think the record companies should take on a more caring and protective role. I was lucky. Around me when I first started were not only wise parents, but mature and responsible people who genuinely wanted what was best for me in every sense. Today I don't think many of those people exist. From what I can make out, record companies make their stars and almost revel and share in their self-indulgence. How much benefit would there be, I wonder, if a company took at least a degree of responsibility for its protégés outside the studio as well as inside. You can't press the parallel too far, I know, but a soccer manager would have stern words for any team player who stepped out of line between matches. He wouldn't dictate behaviour, but he'd certainly demand discipline – and I'd love a record company to have courage enough to take a leaf from that book. Imagine an artist contract, for instance, that said: 'No drugs, or end of deal'! An intrusion into personal liberty, or a practical stand against a social evil? I know what I think.

The other industry cop-out concerns some of the product they help create. There's been a colossal hoo-hah over the kind of literature that gets into children's hands but, I tell you, I've seen singles bags and album covers directed knowingly at a teenage market that would fit well in a Soho porn shop.

Again, to be fair, it's the so-called 'indie' companies, rather than the majors like EMI or CBS, who put out most of the moral garbage, but not always, and it's self-evident that what's recorded on vinyl today would make record men of even ten years ago reluctant to admit their past!

If we aimed at an adult market it may be more defensible on the grounds of mature discernment and all that, but a large chunk of the pop industry's income is from children – neither mature nor discerning. Take away the buying power of the under-eighteens and the record industry as we know it today would feel the draught. Yet, consciously and deliberately, that vulnerable and susceptible market is being fed with what is barely disguised anarchy.

In journalism there's a Press Council which, in theory at least, acts as an industry watchdog to ensure standards of accuracy and honesty. It's a largely toothless body, it seems to me, but at least it does exist. In the music industry there is no equivalent. No watchdog, no restraining influence, no limits – other than the law of the land. If there's a buck to be made, you sail as close to the wind as possible and to heck with who gets hurt in the process, even if it's someone's ten-year-old daughter.

Censorship is a dirty word in certain trendy sections of today's society, but I make no apology whatever for asking for some kind of responsible oversight to operate within the pop business. My contention is that, if a child has mud thrown at him, he'll get dirty. In other art forms we endeavour to shield youngsters from the worst of the muck. Not so in music; the kids are in our sights, and we let fly.

I'm well aware that not everyone shares my belief in moral absolutes, and that to legislate morality is fraught with difficulty. One man's meat, as they say, may be another man's poison, but a 'no holds barred, anything goes' policy can work only in a wholly caring responsible society. It will never work here, nor anywhere else, because people are basically selfish and real freedom can exist only within the framework of rules.

I wonder what all those loud protesters at the time of the car seatbelt legislation have to say in the light of subsequent statistics. An intrusion upon personal liberty, they claimed, yet today it's a proven fact that thousands of lives – including my own – have been saved because wearing a seatbelt was made compulsory. Sure, it would have been better if every driver and passenger had belted up of their own accord. It would have saved a lot of time, effort and money, but I for one needed the incentive of the law and the threat of a fine to make it a habit. And if that was an intrusion on my liberty, then I welcome it, together with any other 'intrusion' designed to protect and keep me alive!

And what's so different about moral safety, where we're equally, if not much more, vulnerable? Here's one artist who would be far more proud of his industry if it wiped its tapes of all the sordid back-door rubbish and remembered it was in the business of entertainment – nothing more pretentious or disturbing than that!

4 DEDICATED FOLLOWERS

4 DEDICATED FOLLOWERS

It's kind of awesome to know that around the world there are thousands of Cliff fans who, given the slightest opportunity, exhibit the most incredible loyalty. Some have been around for as long as my career, others seem to have been weaned on Cliff Richard records and knew 'Living Doll' (original version) backwards by the time they were three. 'I'm six years old and Mummy says I can marry you when I'm grown up,' wrote one child with impeccable taste. 'PS,' she added, 'Mummy thinks that having you as a son-in-law is better than nothing'!

Of course fans have vastly varying degrees of commitment – from those who lash out occasionally on a favourite single to those who turn up at concert after concert, never seem to get bored, buy every Cliff record released, including all the compilations, support me with their cheque books no matter what the charity, shower me with flowers until home often resembles a florist's shop window, and defend me with sharpened nails, if need be, against the knockers and cynics. They're a fantastic group of people, and in all honesty I can't believe many other artists can boast such a responsible and dedicated following.

How much money *Tear Fund* has received from my fans, whether from individuals or groups, I have no idea, but it's certainly many many thousands of pounds, and there must be many thousands of children in Third World countries who are being sponsored on a regular long-term basis by those thoughtful caring people. And what makes me especially proud is that, in most instances, their charity efforts have nothing to do with pleasing or impressing me. Usually I'm kept in the dark, and it's only when I read a report in a local paper or someone whispers in my ear that I have any inkling of all the sponsored walks, fund-raising discos, toy collections, scanner appeals, or whatever, that are initiated by fans, so I'll grab this opportunity to pay tribute and say thanks.

I find it very rewarding and humbling, too, when many of these socially alert people write to say that it was a Cliff gospel concert or church meeting that first sparked off their commitment and enthusiasm. To know that some have taken seriously the beliefs and attitudes I've shared, and have taken them on board personally and independently, is wonderful, and it makes me acutely aware of the huge, and largely untapped and unharnessed, source of energy and power that exists among young people who are out-and-out pop fans.

Bob Geldof's *Live Aid* and *Band Aid* have already given a hint of the potential, but these were commitments by vast numbers to basically one-off events or projects. What about leadership from our pop artists that constructively influences the lives and priorities of their fans on a daily and long-term basis? Like it or not, the pop world communicates more effectively and more loudly to young people than virtually all other message-givers. Parental wisdom is invariably taken with a pinch of salt. Schools, it seems to me, are having their authority and influence deliberately undermined and eroded, while the church's voice, despite some worthwhile and effective influence here and there, remains largely inaudible and irrelevant. But *there* all the time is the pop world, with its millions of tuned-in ears and hungry minds.

Bob Geldof marvellously touched a spark of idealism but, as I say, never saw his role, I guess, as fanning the spark into an ongoing fire. For the most part, pop's conscious influence is limited to the relative trivia of dance styles and hair-dos, while many of the industry moguls – understandably, I suppose – appear to concern themselves exclusively with greater hype and maximum profits.

Again, I know there are exceptions, but in the main the only performers who appear interested in moulding life-styles and values are the so-called 'alternative' acts, who to my mind seem to preach a nightmare world where good is bad and bad is virtue. Somehow we let them get away with it. Yet at least they have a message, and in a sense I have more in common with them than with the artist who shrugs off all responsibility to fans both on as well as off stage. It makes life easier to grab the money and run, but it's an awful waste!

For me, responsibility implies attempting to reflect a

lifestyle, both as a pop singer and as a private individual, which to my way of thinking is worthwhile and desirable. That means sharing my faith as often as I can and making it clear that, while rock 'n' roll is fun, entertaining and enjoyable, and certainly not necessarily shackled to drugs and sex, it's by no means life's pinnacle! In terms of what is profoundly and eternally important, current musical trends and preoccupations are all pretty pathetic and insignificant – compared to what Jesus can mean in a life.

Those who are offended by Christianity are likely to regard that as indoctrination, taking unfair advantage of a public platform. It's OK to proclaim some extreme left-wing ideology or to encourage an 'If it feels good, do it' approach, but dare to hint at a Christian solution, and watch the temperatures soar! Besides which, the old garbage of Christian indoctrination is a non-starter, virtually a contradiction in terms. It doesn't work that way. A person's step into the Christian life is between the individual and the Lord, and no one else. I'm thrilled and amazed to have been instrumental in some of the preliminary steps, but I can never be the *reason* for a fan's conversion. They have to become Christians because they see their need, admit their sin, and accept the way out for themselves. Many people can be used to point the way, and that's great, but Christian conversion isn't about mouthing words or reciting a magic formula, and I fall over backwards to make that clear.

Sometimes people notice that I tend to 'disappear' from certain Christian rallies and meetings before the end. It isn't always that I'm fed up or want to escape the crowds, rather it's to make sure that no one responds to a 'Christian invitation' for the wrong reasons. There will always be some in a big crowd who will jump at the chance to come forward to take a closer squint at me. The cynics don't have to tell me that – I know it, and I do my best not to let it happen. Of course there will still be 'fake' conversions – commitments made with ulterior motives that turn out to be hollow and meaningless. There's no way I can stop the few from mindlessly jumping on the Christian bandwagon, but within weeks they'll have fallen off, bruised and a little disillusioned maybe, but none the worse for wear. What the cynics fail to explain are the fans whose lives are revolutionised by Christ and who discover that being a Cliff Richard fan is still fun, but now incidental. That gives me very great pleasure, and the best fan correspondence is the sort that says, 'Thanks – you've helped me get my life in perspective.'

Talking of correspondence, it's hard, I know, for people to accept that I can't possibly reply personally to their enquiries and requests. For the person who writes, often with painstaking care and effort, their letter is a one-off, probably the only one written that day or that week. For me, it's one of a daily sackful that pours into the office, to home, to the record company, theatre, or wherever. The actual address is irrelevant: 'Cliff Richard, England' seems enough to get through. And, to be brutally honest, I rarely see them, let alone read them. No matter which doormat it drops on, all my mail ends up in the office, where an overworked secretary does her best to keep on top of it all.

Unlike many management offices, we do at least try to acknowledge most of the mail we receive, and, assuming I'm home-based, barely a week goes by without my having to be virtually chained down to tackle the latest pile of autograph requests. Even so, we occasionally receive irate letters from supposed fans, furious that their letters to me have been 'waylaid'. I'm sorry, but that's exactly what secretaries are paid for!

Personally, I don't like letters – either writing them or receiving them – but even if I had a passion for the postbag and was on the doorstep each morning to welcome it, there's no way I could deal with the mail and pursue a career at the same time. Of course all those disappointed scribes must realise that in their heads, but – like the one autograph-hunter in a packed room – the heart hopes there'll somehow be just the one exception. How often have I heard that plea: 'Just me, go on, just me!'

The letters we do take most seriously (although again I can't answer them myself) are those from obviously sincere and occasionally desperate people who are seeking practical and spiritual help. At first it surprised me that people should look to me for advice on what are often sad and complex problems. Again, many of those letters require not only time, but expertise and experience that I don't begin to have. Personal counselling is a fantastic and vital gift, and we therefore direct such mail to Christian friends who have it. (Please see my note on p. 142.) Many people have been helped over the years, I know, by these patient and caring counsellors who answer letters on my behalf. Maybe initially there's disappointment that Cliff Richard doesn't reply himself, but the way I look at it, if the problem is genuine the source of help doesn't matter in the slightest.

I remember a time when we boasted the biggest fan club in Britain, but in the mid-sixties, when I planned to quit show business after becoming a Christian, we dismantled it and there's never been an official one since. Inevitably, I suppose, there have been various attempts to get one going, often by well-meaning people oblivious to all the tax, VAT and business implications. On occasions I've had to bail out naive youngsters who'd received 'out of the blue' tax demands. In the light of those experiences, we adopted our policy of 'no official fan club'.

What's happened since is that seemingly dozens of 'meeting houses' have sprung up in various parts of the country, along with a handful of 'unofficial' clubs. Unofficial in the sense that they have no formal endorsement from me or my management. That's no major drawback, it seems, and we're as helpful as we can be in supplying news and information to whoever asks. In a sense that's a much better set-up, because my fans aren't part of any high-powered business with profit motives or accountants looking over their shoulders.

The disadvantage – and it frustrates me no end – is the squabbling that seems to flare up every so often between one group and another. If the qualification for a fan is to like what I do, the last thing I want is pointless rivalry. A funny thing, human nature.

I must admit there's an element about the whole fan scene that I've never quite understood and have certainly never enjoyed. I think it's the hallmark of the peripheral fan rather than the genuine one, and it's sort of summed up in the attitude: 'We put you where you are, so you owe us.' Usually it bubbles to the surface after I fail to sign an autograph or can't comply with some particular request. The assumption seems to be that for twenty-four hours every day I'm public property and have some duty to be constantly smiling and permanently available.

Just recently in a restaurant I was about to sip a spoonful of hot soup when my arm was shoved from behind and a menu landed by the plate. 'Sign that,' I was ordered. My promise to do so when I'd finished my meal didn't go down too well with the phantom arm-shover, and I got the usual 'We made you . . .' line.

For the most part, although it's hard to excuse the bad manners, I reckon it has to be a mixture of nervousness and alcohol that spawns that kind of abrasive attitude. She wouldn't have been a real fan, I hasten to add, and her Cliff record collection probably amounted to an album she was given twenty years ago and never liked. But to those who believe that buying a record or attending a concert entitles them to some share in public ownership of the artist, may I blow the sweetest of raspberries. The truth is, if the public don't like my next piece of work they won't buy it; if they do, then hopefully they will. And of course that's exactly how it should be. It's the same with your greengrocer: if you like what he sells, you'll go again; if you don't, you'll buy your spuds from someone else.

At the dinner-table I reckon I'm reasonably tolerant, and I confess I've caught myself before now interrupting a conversation to say 'Hi!' to someone I admire and happen to bump into in a restaurant. Hopefully though, I do so with a bit more courtesy and a better sense of timing.

Even worse for me than the arm-shovers are the car-chasers. They really do annoy me, and I know I've upset and probably disillusioned quite a few drivers and passengers by being downright crotchety.

Perhaps I over-react, but as soon as I'm aware of being followed – and I've developed a sixth sense by now – I feel the hackles rise. To my way of thinking, I've done my work. I've probably spent twenty minutes or so at the stage door, signing autographs for everyone who asks – I certainly did that virtually every night for a year after *Time* – and after that the last thing I want is my privacy invaded by fans pursuing me to where I'm going to eat, probably with family or friends. When I was twenty and we were smuggled out of theatres through back doors, it was all somehow different. Now I'm past that stage and I feel the need for some semblance of dignity. Maybe the fans enjoy the thrill of a street chase. Usually I don't give them that pleasure. What they do get is an emergency stop and me jumping out to deliver a sharp flea in the ear. So much for image building!

Sadly, there are a few whose lives and thinking sometimes shift alarmingly out of gear. Cliff Richard becomes a total obsession, and whole lives revolve around where I am and what I do. That's disturbing for me, simply because it's so destructive for them. Most times, I'm relieved to say, the obsession passes and real-life romance wipes out the preoccupation and the fantasy.

I had a smashing letter, for instance, from a group of regulars who came by coach to one of my shows a while back. 'We know you must think we're all potty, but we honestly don't think about you all the time – only when we get together and can share the same interest. Actually you're just our favourite hobby!' That's how I love it to be, and I only wish I had some answer or remedy for the comparative handful whose minds have played tricks and who live in their disturbing make-believe worlds.

In any one week I'm likely to have a dozen letters or more – accusing me of fathering children by women I've never heard of, or demanding money I'm supposed to owe to total strangers – and sometimes I even receive parcels with really unpleasant contents. Once I received a dead bird, with various voodoo signs and threats.

Items through the mail are easily disposed of. Deranged people on the doorstep are more difficult to handle. One lady, whom I'd never set eyes on before, arrived in a taxi, with several items of luggage, and announced she was my fiancée and had come to stay, as arranged. Luckily the taxi driver was persuaded to take her away.

'The Lord' has apparently directed a number of folk to my house for no apparent reason, at least not evident to me, and if it weren't for the fact that they're so persistent and pathetic, and genuinely seem to believe in their 'voices', it would all be quite hilarious. Not so with the burly woman from Holland who was intent on tearing my hair out for a cause I never quite fathomed. She succeeded in leaving me with some hefty welts across the face before Bill Latham and I were driven to the indignity of quite literally having to sit on her until the police arrived. She's the only one, to my knowledge, whose threats resulted in Interpol's involvement.

By comparison, the lady who's been roaming around my garden at night for virtually twenty years – and who seems to want nothing more than to watch room lights go on and off – is harmless, and we've given up worrying about her. Bill often shouts 'Goodnight' in the direction of a gloomy patch of rhododendron bushes, convinced she's lurking somewhere behind.

There are others, from the almost daily nutty phone calls that the office secretary has to endure, to the woman whose complex fantasy was apparently triggered when I once smiled in her direction from stage.

I know I'm not alone in attracting the mentally unstable. Every 'celebrity' has his or her fair share, I'm sure, but, as I say, it's disturbing to encounter so many sick people so regularly, and it gives me food for thought that I might be responsible for, or – perhaps more accurately – might be the focus of their delusions. I haven't a clue what to do about it, and I dread to think what a field day the press would have with some of the allegations and incidents if only they knew of them. I can see the headlines now: 'Cliff Struggles With Girl At Gate.' You can understand why we keep our distance and why it's very rare indeed for me to allow a fan relationship to become a friendship.

Yet for me too it's essential that I keep a proper perspective, and when I see from on stage that great sea of enthusiastic waving arms and hear the cheers of the fans (some of whom travel regularly from Europe, Japan, America and even Australia for a British concert), all the personal hassles – which I've long since accepted as par for the course – somehow become more manageable. 'If you don't like the heat,' they say, 'get out of the kitchen.' That's just it. While the fans keep coming, I'll risk the occasional burn.

5 SORRY, I DON'T WEAR ONE!

5 SORRY, I DON'T WEAR ONE!

A while back I had an interview arranged with a health magazine. Presumably I was to be written up as a shining example of radiant health in mid life! I turned up for the interview with a runny nose, a thumping headache and blocked sinuses. Photographs were postponed until another day, and I snuffled and spluttered through the inquisition, painfully aware that I must have looked a ghastly disappointment.

Funnily enough, I rarely catch colds – at least not bad ones – but that was a right snorter and I surely demolished the 'Peter Pan of Pop' myth for at least one writer with a single blow of the nose. But while I readily confess that the 'ever youthful' image becomes increasingly difficult to live up to by the year – and, believe me, there are days when I feel more like Peter Pan's grandad – I'm very aware too of the importance of looking and feeling good, and I'm positive the two are linked.

No one would describe me as a health or fitness fanatic, and I certainly don't have any secret recipes for staying young or for dodging marauding germs and viruses. But I do take good health seriously and endeavour to treat my body with the respect it demands. I'm grateful for the fact that I'm not a naturally 'sickly' person. I never have been, so I can't imagine what it must be like to be confined to bed for any length of time, or to face some long-term disability.

I don't exactly take good health for granted, but I don't mooch around half-expecting to be poorly tomorrow either! Obviously there's a whole load still to discover about the connection between our state of mind and actual physical health. Some people pooh-pooh the idea of mind over matter, but not me. Although I guess I was fortunate to inherit an optimistic temperament and a fairly positive approach to life, I don't think we pay nearly as much attention to our moods and attitudes as we should. I know there's a rather dubious and American-orientated philos-ophy built up around Norman Vincent Peale's *Power Of Positive Thinking*, and I feel there are times when it is wise to recognise and acknowledge our own vulnerability and limitations. But at the same time I'm sure we could do ourselves a power of good by expecting the best for a change, rather than the typically British but dangerously corrosive attitude of being prepared for the worst! If you're geared up for the worst, life has a nasty habit of delivering just that.

There's no way I could have survived three decades in the entertainment business and in public life if I'd even *thought* about, let alone half expected, failure. Even today I'm still convinced, genuinely convinced, that my best album is yet to come. I know I could do a much better job in a musical than *Time* ever permitted, and in due course I'll do it. And even on the tennis court I reckon there's a lot more potential to realise before the old creaking joints surrender completely.

The point is that, for me at least, targets – or ambitions, if you like – are crucial. Not the impossible *Fantasy Island* kind, but realistic attainable targets which channel your energy and challenge your mind. 'Go For It' is the simple slogan on the desk of a pastor friend of mine. That's my kind of philosophy. Perhaps, as I say, my temperament makes it relatively easy.

'It's OK for him,' I can hear people say, emerging from their day-dreams, 'he's made that way.' But I'm positive all of us are capable of setting our sights on worthwhile targets, even though it means we may have to work for them and sometimes discipline ourselves in the process.

I have a recurring back problem, so, to prevent a disc from popping out and causing agony, I work hard at strengthening the muscles around the spine. Every morn-ing I do a session of sit-ups and back pulls and, although it's a chore, I know it will help prevent trouble ahead.

Yet, although we're used to a bit of hard grind in one form or another to keep our bodies in good shape, it seldom occurs to us that our minds need similar care and attention. If thinking positively and constructively has been just one factor that's helped me steer clear of depressions or anxieties, then that's a health tip worth cultivating.

Talking of physical exercises, by the way, I'm really not

into any kind of rigorous routine, other than that morning work-out which takes about ten or fifteen minutes on the bedroom carpet. As well as helping the back, as I've said, the sit-ups strengthen the tummy muscles, ensuring that the midriff sits under the belt rather than hangs over it!

Once upon a time I did begin some Nautilus training at a gymnasium, but I discovered that that's only helpful if you maintain it on a regular basis. If you're erratic, as my schedule virtually guarantees, your muscles just can't cope. Besides which, I found it painful and boring – exactly the same problem I discovered with jogging. That didn't last long either. I console myself with the thought that my concerts must be the equivalent of a good two-hour work-out, and if I don't get at least six hours' thrash a week on the tennis court I sense the onset of withdrawal symptoms.

Seriously, when Sue Barker got me heavily into tennis in the early Eighties, it was one of the best favours ever. Before I met Sue, I played tennis a little, but it was more social than sporty, and my standard was pathetic – typical recreation park pat-a-cake stuff. Meeting real players on the professional circuit changed all that, and their standard of play, fitness and commitment to the game was an inspiration.

Since then I've joined two major tennis clubs, had scores of lessons from very patient coaches, and spent countless hours just practising. In a practice session you're likely to hit a thousand balls, whereas in a game it's probably nearer two hundred. I've no delusions about reaching any brilliant standard – or entering Wimbledon, as one naive newspaperman seriously enquired. I just want to be as good as possible, so I can extract every ounce of enjoyment. There's tremendous satisfaction in knowing you've hit a ball just right and with perfect timing, and, strangely enough, it's nothing to do with having to win. I'm really not that competitive, and some of the most enjoyable tennis of all is playing with a friend of mine whom I've never beaten, but who draws the best out of me – and I know that I'm making him work increasingly hard for the games he wins.

Again it's back to the mental aspect. Contrary to general belief, my work can often be highly stressful, as well as ruthlessly demanding. Tight schedules, press interviews and unrelenting public attention frequently crash together and produce heavy pressure situations. That's when an

67

hour's hit on a tennis court is the best psychotherapy imaginable. Out goes all aggression and frustration and, although nothing changes at work, I at least feel more relaxed and equipped to cope with it.

I've gained so much from tennis – in terms of both fitness and enjoyment – that it's been great to give a bit back to the game by way of my annual Pro-Celebrity Tournament. We've held five so far, all at The Brighton Centre, just prior to Christmas. And, at least as far as the UK is concerned, and possibly even the world, they're unique. A mix of hilarious comedy from the likes of Mike Yarwood, Ronnie Corbett and Peter Cook, with a sprinkling of competitive tennis from enthusiasts such as Emlyn Hughes, Elton John, Mike Read and Terry Wogan, have ensured sell-out attendances. And, for the tennis purists, the involvement of our top women professionals – for instance, Virginia Wade, Sara Gomer, Annabel Croft and Sue Barker – means there's the added flash of genuine class! It's a really fun, friendly evening, and, at the end of it, I've now been inveigled into leading some impromptu carol-singing to the accompaniment of the local Salvation Army band.

The icing on the cake is that so far we've been able to hand over well in excess of £100,000 to the Lawn Tennis Association to assist in finding new talent at real grass-roots, recreation-park level. Unfortunately tennis isn't a cheap game to pursue seriously. Club memberships are expensive, and the kind of intensive coaching that a talented kid would need to bring him or her up to any kind of serious competitive level would cost the parents a small fortune. There are already all sorts of schemes under way which enable grants and free coaching, but, since indoor court facilities in Britain are still very limited (although fast improving, I'm delighted to say), the LTA seemed pleased to grab my initiative and with the Tournament profits – enhanced by generous sponsorship from The Mortgage Corporation – set up the Cliff Richard 'Search For A Star' programme.

From a national programme of all-comers' 'fun days' around the country, boys and girls who, in the opinion of sharp-eyed area coaches, show any sort of potential are selected for further assessment, and an elite handful end up attending a three-day course at Bisham Abbey, the LTA's National Training Centre.

The exciting thing is that already some of these young-sters, who perhaps a year before hadn't a clue which end of a racquet was which, are making their mark on junior leagues and tournaments. Who knows, one of these days one of them may emerge as Britain's answer to Boris Becker or Steffi Graf – and those who've written us off as a nation of tennis wimps will be revising their opinions!

So those of you who'd never be seen at a Cliff concert, how about watching me play tennis one year at Brighton? I wish I could say I'm the current Tournament champion, but I've just lost it! Sometimes I wonder about the lack of justice in this world . . .

Emotionally, in fact, I don't reckon I'm a very up or down person. I rarely wake up either desperately gloomy or hysterically happy, which, as well as making for peaceful breakfasts, casts a bit of doubt on the credibility of my biolator. If you're not into biolators, I'd better explain.

Basically it's nothing more than a pocket calculator adapted to work out your biorhythms, which you knew all the time! I picked mine up in Tokyo years ago and, although I'm not a hundred percent convinced, it does have an uncanny knack of being right.

The basic idea is that, from the time we're born, our bodies are affected by the various energies that hit our earth from the sun and the moon. These, reasonably enough, are said to occur in regular cycles and affect us physically, emotionally and intellectually. These cycles are respec-tively twenty-three days, twenty-eight days and thirty-three days. For half of those periods we're apparently on 'highs' or at our best; for the other half we're on 'lows' or at our most vulnerable. Particularly critical are the 'cross-over' days. By simply punching up your date of birth on the calculator and subtracting the current date, the biolator displays where you're at in your cycle.

Now I don't know more about the theory than that and, though you'll probably conclude it's further evidence of fast-approaching senility, I have a suspicion that there's more to it than meets the eye.

The Japanese are certainly convinced, and many of them take it all so seriously that, if the reading shows a physical low, then it's back to bed – fast. The wiser ones on no account let the thing rule their lives, but they do take notice.

A businessman, for instance, who knows he's on an intellectual low, particularly if it's a critical day, will be extra careful about his decision-making. During an emotional trough, he'll handle relationships more sensitively. And physically critical times rule out unnecessary risks.

Now I'm not that hooked, and there's no way I run my life by a calculator. But on days when I feel a bit out of sorts and the back's grumbling, or I'm conscious of more hassles than usual, I'll often punch up my biorhythms, more out of curiosity than anything else, and, blow me, if nine times out of ten it hasn't shown a critical or low reading. Perhaps it's just coincidence, but if I do see a critical day looming then I'm conscious of being just that little bit more wary.

Be clear about one thing – biorhythms have nothing to do with horoscopes, fortune-telling, or weird and dangerous occult powers. That area isn't for me, I promise you, nor should it be for anyone with a half-ounce of sense. The biorhythms theory may be so much bunkum, but at least it's based on a natural law of the universe. And if one day it is all discredited, then the worst that has happened is that some of us have been more cautious at times than really necessary – and that's no bad thing!

Whereas biorhythms are largely about speculation, the connection between Christianity and health certainly isn't. Sometimes people within the church are amazingly naive about Christians getting ill. They seem to think that Christian faith brings with it some magical immunity from every bug and infection that happens to be around. Presumably, therefore, if two guys, one a Christian and one not, happen to be exposed to the same germ, it would be the non-believer who would get zapped.

That really is as hideous an idea as it is daft – although, sad to say, there are a growing number of Christians who have latched on to this belief, and whose only answer to sickness and disease when it strikes at a Christian is that somewhere along the line the person's faith has been deficient. How they explain away the Old Testament story of Job I can't imagine. Whether that's a kind of parable or a historical account, I don't know. For me it doesn't matter. The truth it teaches is plain – that, whereas it's no part of God's plan or character to cause suffering and pain, there is another power at work on this earth that is wholly destructive, and that's Satan.

The story of Job is simply that God permitted his suffering to reassure us that, no matter how terrible the adversity, no matter how scarred we might become in life, God is still in control and shares our pain and our grief with a love that I guess we'll never understand until we're with him in eternity.

When I opened my mouth in the middle of that gospel concert tour in 1985 and swallowed a throat virus, that was it! No more singing for eight weeks, and a trail of several thousand very disappointed people. Was it because I'd offended God and this was some sort of punishment? Why in the middle of gospel concerts, when we were specifically doing his work? What dreadful blind alleys you lurch into once you embark on that sort of inquest.

Similarly, when I aquaplaned at sixty miles an hour into the car in front of me on the M4 and wrote off a new VW Golf, of course I was grateful to God that I scrambled out with nothing more than a stiff neck, but I'm honestly not sure whether I can say it was God's protection. I was OK because I was sensible enough to be wearing my seat-belt. Without it I'd have been through the windscreen for sure.

Before all you Christian charismatics write me off as a spiritual wimp, I'm not suggesting for one moment that Christianity has no bearing on our health – far from it. The very essence of our faith is that God is concerned for us as whole people – our minds, bodies and souls. His desire is that we should be fit in all departments. But we're not puppets. When we become Christians, we're not swathed in heavenly cotton wool and protected from all that's nasty or threatening.

The Christian life is a partnership, with a good chunk of the responsibility fairly and squarely on our shoulders. The Bible leaves not the slightest doubt that it's *me* who is responsible for *my* body. It is the 'temple of the Holy Spirit' and I'm to treat it with respect and care, and do my utmost, if you like, to supply him with a piece of machinery that works.

So, yes, I will make sure I wear a seat-belt when driving, and, no, I'm not going to fill my lungs with poisonous nicotine or pump myself full of some drug which I know will cause damage. I can understand the need for some non-believers to look for their kicks in drug-taking and all manner of extremes. Many artists in show business are completely fulfilled people while they're on stage, but off it their lives are empty. And of course they'll look for gratification wherever it's available. It's fantastic for me when I hear about colleagues in the business discovering that a relationship with Christ gives them all the kicks and highs they could ever cope with.

Yet I don't want to give the impression that all Christians are paragons of virtue when it comes to looking after themselves. We have a lot to learn, I tell you. I wonder, for instance, what right the Christian has to heap criticism on the drug user, while he continues to shovel more and more calories into an already fat and overweight body. Hardly the way to ensure the efficient functioning of God's handiwork, I would have thought. Suffice it to say that I've no desire whatsoever to be like some of the slovenly looking Christians I've met. Rather than walking advertisements for the faith, they're in danger of being slouching deterrents.

I hope it doesn't sound too smug, but at least in the area of eating and dieting I reckon I've got it just about right – although it was merely ego that prompted my first dietary blitz early in my career. It's a well-documented story. Minnie Caldwell, a character in *Coronation Street*, referred in one episode to 'that chubby Cliff Richard', and that did it. I looked in the mirror, and she was right. Two stones overweight at least, and it was time to take myself in hand. I reckoned if animals could survive on just one meal a day then so could I.

From then on I gradually weaned myself off those marvellous cooked breakfasts and three-course lunches, and concentrated on one main evening meal. And, by and large, that's been the pattern ever since. For some, I'm sure, it isn't the right way, and I know the experts would frown on the idea of major food intake late at night, although I do start the day with a couple of slices of brown toast and a cup of tea. But for me it works, and obviously it fits in with my lifestyle. I could never go on stage in the evening and leap around with a full stomach, so it's late-night eating more often than not.

The great thing about one meal a day is that I'm not worried about a diet as such. A man can take in up to 2,500 calories a day, but it would be a hefty old meal that provided that lot. So what I eat is no great problem,

72

although I do tend to be a bit cagey about red meat. That's certainly the hardest to digest at night and if it's fatty, then I'd rather not be tempted. I'm not too bothered about it after an active day of tennis or whatever, but on the whole I favour white meats, and, on tour especially, I'm careful to vary my meals as much as possible. Chicken one night, fish another, an omelette maybe, and a couple of nights a week I'll stick to veggies only.

Just as a word of caution, I'd better add that, if anyone plans a drastic food reduction – and I reckon we'd all manage perfectly well, and probably better, on one meal a day – you should check with the doctor about compensating for any essential vitamins you might be losing. Obviously if you cut out a meal you're cutting out vitamins, so I swig down a daily multi-vitamin capsule, the mega variety, as well as a kelp tablet for the barnet, and a royal jelly capsule for just about everything else! Don't ask me what royal jelly does. All I know is that the queen bee makes it and all the little worker bees feed off it for their energy. It obviously doesn't do them any harm, and it's given me a passable buzz for quite some years!

But back to the ego. I have a sneaking suspicion that, if one ghastly night the teeth and hair fell out and the face wrinkled like an old prune, I'd be first in line for cosmetic surgery. Hopefully it can't happen like that, and I've no qualms about ageing gracefully in front of people. I'll never convince some that I really haven't had a nose job or the creases ironed out.

There's another popular rumour that's always bewildered me, and I never quite know how to handle it. After all, how do you convince someone that you don't wear a colostomy bag? It would be a sick joke, were it not for dozens of gentle and lovely letters I receive from folk who've had this drastic surgery, thanking me for the 'incredible example' I've been to them. 'If you can lead such an active life,' they say, 'it shows what can be done.' You see what I mean? It's hard to disillusion people like that, and all I can do is ask the medical profession, please, to let it be known that I've never had the operation and have no idea where the story started.

What ailments I do have, for anyone morbid enough to be interested, are a dodgy back, which I've told you about; a tendency towards kidney stones – I carry around some dynamite-strength pain-killers just in case; an irritating tennis elbow, which surfaced just as I endorsed a pamphlet for the Arthritis Council; and all-too-apparent short-sightedness.

I hated wearing glasses at first, but I was only eleven, and kids are more sensitive. As I got older, I cared less about the specs and more about wanting to see properly. On stage they're a drag and I leave them behind in the dressing-room. It's better to risk a tumble into the orchestra pit than to see those expensive frames disappearing off the nose in a cascade of sweat. And, yes, I've tried contact lenses many times, but never found any that were comfortable and didn't feel like having half of Brighton beach in the eyeball. Persevere a bit longer, say the opticians, and you'll get used to them. Personally, I don't think I ever will.

Coping with a duff back and the possibility of kidney stones is largely common-sense. When I lift heavy things I try to be conscious of doing it the right way, bending the knees and all that, and when I do get the slightest twinge in the spine I pull the mattress off the bed and take to the floor for a few nights. Well, at least that's what I used to do. While I was filming for *Tear Fund* in Kenya I found this great wood-slatted unsprung bed, which I bought and had shipped home. Now the mattress stays put and every night I'm quite literally in good shape.

Gulping down five or six pints of water is the antidote to kidney problems, but since taking a daily dose of homeopathic medicine, which apparently breaks down any potential stone, the problem hasn't recurred. I'm grateful – the pain of one of those stones on the move is murderous.

For Christians and non-Christians alike, the whole question of faith healing – or, more accurately, divine healing – is a controversial issue. Within the Christian church there are thousands who could give positive testimony to God's miraculous healing. On the other hand, there are equal numbers whose condition has remained unchanged despite faith, prayer, the laying on of hands, and even fasting. My own experience is limited to a private meeting with a Christian healer when my back was troublesome.

At the time, after prayer, it seemed as though my right leg, which was fractionally shorter than the left, grew a little. With hindsight, I'm just not sure. Perhaps I imagined it. My back still grumbles a little, but it's never been really bad since. Perhaps God did intervene and there was a miracle. Perhaps at the same time I had to be sensible and exercise regularly to strengthen the muscles.

What I *am* sure about is that in some instances God can and does override, sometimes very dramatically, and people are healed. The New Testament leaves us in no doubt whatsoever, and today there is overwhelming evidence from all around the world that God is still a God who heals. But the bottom line is that *he* decides and thereby hangs *our* problem. Why does he choose to heal one and not another? Why did he allow an outstanding Christian leader like David Watson to die of cancer at a relatively young age, when there was a whole army of Christians praying for his recovery? I have no answer. And why, of all the engagements I had in 1985, did it have to be my gospel tour that was disrupted by a throat virus? Again, there was so much prayer for a rapid recovery, but nothing. If anything, the throat got worse and there were more cancellations.

Just think of the dilemma in Jesus' day. He healed blind men, lepers, the woman who was haemorrhaging, a man who'd been paralysed for thirty years, a man with a withered hand, and so on. An incredible demonstration of God's power and compassion. But what about the other equally deserving – maybe from our perspective even more deserving – victims of sickness and disease? There must have been thousands of them who never got a look-in, or were simply pushed aside in the crush. Why didn't Jesus have time for them?

I know that for many that's a real hindrance to faith, because from our viewpoint it all seems just a little unfair. But that's from our viewpoint, which is human and limited to our puny understanding of time and space.

There's a well-known little book by J. B. Phillips called *Your God Is Too Small*, and that title exactly explains the mistake we make. We expect God to think as we do, to agree with us as to what's best for our welfare, and to back our judgement as to who are the good guys and the not so good. We want God to be like us, but mercifully he isn't. The simple and obvious truth is that God knows better than I do. I don't understand why he chooses to heal some and not others, but who am I to question the God who created every star and planet in the universe? Sure, I'm puzzled about David Watson and having to cancel gospel concerts, and a hundred and one other things, but they don't shake my faith, because I know that not only is God in control but, despite all the problems and paradoxes, he actually loves me. The Bible says that in this life we 'see but a poor reflection as in a mirror'. That's how it is. So much is obscured and confused, but we're promised that one day the mirror's reflection will disappear and our mind's eye will understand, and one of the first revelations, I'm sure, will be that everything, no matter how painful at the time, was for our good after all.

6 SINGLE-MINDED

6 SINGLE-MINDED

At the time it seemed a good idea. A chapter on being single and how I coped might possibly help and encourage other 'unmarrieds' who are viewing permanent 'on the shelf' status with mixed feelings. Nearly fifty years of self-sufficiency ought to have taught me something worth sharing! It was a suggestion I couldn't ignore – particularly as it came from my publisher. Yet what a headache it was when it came to putting thoughts on paper.

After an hour of platitudes and waffle, I was tempted to scrap it, but suddenly the problem surfaced. The problem was that I hadn't got a problem, and I was trying to write as though I had! Sorry if that's double Dutch – I'd better explain.

For me, being single isn't a drag or a pressure. It doesn't cause dark depression or make me lie awake bemoaning what might have been. I really doubt if I'm a bundle of sexual hang-ups and frustrations. In a nutshell, I actually enjoy being single! And there I was, trying to explain how I coped with it, as though it was some appalling handicap or deformity.

So I wiped out the waffle and platitudes and started again, this time altogether more positively, on how to enjoy being single. And immediately I ran into another brick wall. Again it took a while to see what was wrong, and, to be honest, when the light did dawn, it was a difficult admission. But the more I thought, the more I realised that my perspective on relationships was not only untypical but extremely privileged, and, rather than presume to offer advice to others, the best I could aim for was a spot of self-analysis, an explanation of why *I* enjoy being single. What did I know, for goodness sake, about feeling socially isolated or 'left out', as I realise many unmarrieds do. With a name like mine, there's never a shortage of invitations to parties, dinners, bar mitzvahs – and an increasing number of retirement celebrations! How could I advise people about immersing themselves in work or a hobby, when my career has been unique in terms of reward and opportunity? *Any* advice would seem arrogant and patronising.

So the tape was wiped for a second time, and I started again. No advice, no pat solutions, just my findings, take them or leave them. And, incidentally, no defence – especially no defence. How many times have I kicked myself for falling into the trap of defending the fact that I'm single? You've heard the question, with the not-so-subtle innuendo, 'Why haven't you married then?' Maybe single people should start reversing the tables. 'Why on earth did you get married?' That would flummox a few!

Then there's the other equally irritating approach: 'Haven't you ever thought about settling down?' The fact is that I'm probably vastly more 'settled down' than the questioner, whose marital record is, odds on, a shambles. I suppose that line of interrogation poses for me the nearest thing approaching a 'pressure'. It's amazing how so many people's minds just can't grasp that the single man or woman isn't necessarily inadequate, gay or abnormal, and that it's actually possible to pursue a single lifestyle perfectly happily, healthily, and without experiencing appalling deprivation.

So, let me tell you why I'm content as I am, with apologies to those who'll be offended at the very thought of anyone being content about anything!

At the risk of sounding like a preacher with a three-point sermon, I discover that there really are three main contentment ingredients, and all of them, would you believe, begin with the same letter.

The first is *fulfilment*, and whether it's temperament, make-up, genes or plain old job satisfaction I don't know, but I've never 'missed' having a wife in the sense of being envious of those who have. Neither, strangely enough, do I feel cheated in any way by not having children. I say 'strangely', because I love kids and get a fantastic thrill and satisfaction from being uncle to my sisters' children. In all, at the current count, there are ten – six girls and four boys – and I'm close to them all. In my opinion I'm a good uncle, and would probably make an even better dad. I'd certainly be a disciplinarian, but that's another story!

I have no doubt that a major reason for the lack of

Right: 'All these people and I've forgotten my racquet.' Bill Latham, who organises my Tournament each year, copes with a slight problem. *(Photo: Julie Wetzel)*

Below: 'Working out' for Sport Aid with Lulu and Elaine Paige.

This lively bunch are some of the budding tennis champs 'discovered' through the 'Search For A Star' scheme which the Lawn Tennis Association runs with proceeds from the Pro-Celebrity Tournament.

(Photo: Tommy Hindley)

'Now look here, Virginia – just because you won Wimbledon...'   *(Photo: Tommy Hindley)*

Above: A 'blockbuster' of a joke, this one, and radio and TV presenter Bob Holness certainly saw the funny side. I always enjoy a 'live' interview situation, and this one at London's Barbican Theatre was especially good value.

Below: I don't expect one's allowed 'favourite' Royals – but, nevertheless, mine's the Duchess of Kent every time. She's a fabulous lady, and my TIME compatriots – Jodie Wilson, Mike Moran and Dawn Hope – were obviously in full agreement. *(Photo: Featureflash)*

Swimming and cycling, they say, are two of the best forms of exercise. It's years since I took a bike ride but, provided the water's warm and the sun's shining, I'm a reasonable little crawler!

Right: My Portuguese villa offers really strenuous holidays. It's about the only place in the world where I go and do absolutely nothing.

Me and my dog. Emma was a gift from the fans some ten years ago, and she's been seeing off marauding squirrels and burglars ever since! *(Photo: Colin Ramsay)*

Simple exercises to prevent arthritic fingers.

heartache is that there is a colossal and very tangible compensation for family life in my career. People say I'm married to my job, and in a way I suppose I am. It certainly occupies much of my time, thinking and energy. I don't like the term 'workaholic', because that implies addiction. If I had to quit the business, I know I could. But some probably think the label's appropriate, and admittedly I do pack a lot into a year. Although I kid myself that I'd love a long stretch of doing absolutely nothing, I suspect that in no time I'd be sticking my nose into recording studios, offering to do back-up vocals for anybody who'd have me!

By nature I tend to be single-minded about what I tackle and don't really get off on half-measures. Whether it's tennis, my Christian activities, singing, or whatever, there's a hint of the perfectionist about me. That's not necessarily a boast, but a way of saying that I like to be successful and therefore attempt only what I know I can do well and I'm likely to enjoy. What I don't enjoy I usually don't attempt!

It's probably a false rationalisation to say that a career in show business, which has been in virtually permanent top gear for thirty years, could never have run alongside a successful marriage. I'm sure others have made both work, but I do know that both demand enormous investments of time and commitment, and I'm not sure how I could have coped with the two without one or the other suffering. If I'd married, I would have hated my career to get in the way of family relationships. Shamefully, I suspect I may have been equally upset if a wife got in the way of my work!

I don't think there can be anyone in show business who enjoys their career more than I do. Even after all this time I still get a colossal kick when records make the charts and when concert halls are packed out around the country and overseas. To know that one day I could well overtake Elvis as the UK's leading hit-maker is hard to digest, but it's true. At the moment he's still streets ahead, but if my voice holds out and I can still find the right songs, it *is* possible to catch up – and I'm probably the only one of our generation who could.

It's like another world to think back to those four months after leaving school when I was a credit control clerk in a factory in North London. Perhaps I'd have known a totally different kind of fulfilment if I'd stayed there, but it wouldn't have stemmed from work, I'm sure of that. I really do sympathise with those millions of people who are in jobs which give no satisfaction or excitement. I can't imagine going through life dreading Mondays and endlessly watching the clock until 5 p.m. That's why I'm so ill-equipped to give advice. If you're single and work neither absorbs nor stimulates you, then, humanly speaking, I wonder whether fulfilment can possibly be found. Sports and hobbies can surely occupy only a relatively small chunk of life.

I guess this is where temperament plays a part, because, sorry though I am for people whose lives are lonely and a drudgery, I can't imagine that I'd have soldiered through that kind of existence, even if I hadn't made it as a singer. It's said that people fall into one of two categories – those who see problems and those who see possibilities. I'm definitely in the second group, and although I suppose the world needs a balanced mix of both (sometimes I do need people around me to apply the brakes!), I'm an out-and-out believer in the 'go for it' approach. As I say, perhaps it's just a matter of temperament, in which case I'm lucky, but to apply a positive attitude to being single and to recognise its possibilities has to be far preferable to mooning around, diminished by its drawbacks, and hankering after something that may never happen.

And, OK, I acknowledge that there *are* drawbacks. There's the pressure, spoken and unspoken, that comes from being middle-aged and unmarried. Anyone not conforming to majority behaviour patterns finds pressures, and I don't pretend that they're not tiresome. I'm sure my mum, bless her, would like to see me married, although no way would she attempt to 'organise' me into it! But just knowing how she feels is a pressure!

I remember, many years ago when the Shadows were getting married, feeling ever so slightly the 'odd man out' and wanting in a way to conform. What a disastrous motive that would have been for marriage. 'It's expected, therefore I do it' has to have been the recipe for so many heartaches and divorces. All of us must know friends or relatives who've plunged into marriage, almost desperate for married status, yet were anything but ready for commitment. It demands a fair degree of maturity to appreciate that loving someone is more than feeling euphoric, and, that a heck of a lot of sacrifice is required too.

Undoubtedly for me the biggest pressure to marry has come from the media and the so-called 'public image'. If I had a pound for every time a journalist has quizzed me about marriage, I'd have enough for *Tear Fund* to double its aid programme. It would have been much easier, that's for sure, and saved all the mindless speculation about my sexual preferences, if I'd proved the point by tying the proverbial knot.

The questions still come, usually from the tabloid press people, who don't represent genuine newspapers anyway. And they must be as tired of writing the same old answers as I am of giving them. 'Are you going to get married?' 'I've no plans.' 'Why? Are you gay?' I thought my best answer to that one was to a magazine feature writer recently: 'If every middle-aged man who's single is automatically gay, where does that put the Pope?' That shut her up!

I have to admit that once or twice it has crossed my mind that it would be great to be married. But then there are times, too, when I've thought it would be great to live in Australia, or great to play Centre Court, Wimbledon. Many things appeal and are desirable, but reality says you can't have them all! The fact is that I have enormous respect for marriage, and I'd be the last one on earth to approach it flippantly.

That leads to what has to be the biggest fulfilment factor of all – my Christian faith. At the risk of over-simplifying the matter, Christianity has given me a security and a wholeness which I can't imagine could be equalled by any other relationship, philosophy or lifestyle. I can't fully analyse or explain why that should be – I don't want to give the impression that I endorse the 'Come to Jesus and all will be well' mentality. For many, 'coming to Jesus' is when the going really starts to get tough. But what I do know is that Christ's promise to give 'life in all its fulness' is no 'pie in the sky' idealism. For me it works, and instead of writing off Christianity as restrictive and cramping, as many mistakenly do, I've discovered much wider horizons and freedoms since my conversion in the mid-Sixties. Christianity really does reach those parts that a career (however successful), a family (however close), and a temperament (however fortunate), just can't reach when it comes to feeling 'complete'.

To be aware of being known, loved and accepted by the

almighty God, despite all my pathetic failures and selfish tendencies, puts the rest of life in perspective. All of us need to feel loved and wanted, and, take it from me, there's nothing second best about being on the receiving end of God's love. Christ never suggested that his Father's love was any feeble alternative for the bachelors and spinsters of this world, or that it was any kind of heavenly compensation for staying single. What he did explain and demonstrate was that God's love transcends all others, that it's always totally dependable, and always, always available.

I'm not one of those people who litter the place with Bible texts; in fact, although I read the Bible regularly, I've a dreadful memory when it comes to reciting chapter and verse. Nevertheless, here's one worth memorising – Romans 8:38–39. How's this for heart-stirring comfort, even if there's no husband or wife to share your bed?

> For I am convinced that neither death nor life, neither angels nor demons, neither the present nor the future, nor any powers, neither height nor depth, nor anything else in all creation, will be able to separate us from the love of God that is in Christ Jesus our Lord.

With a guarantee like that, I reckon I can get through periods when it's easy to get broody and despondent about staying solo. I'm positive that the more we bring God's love into the centre of our lives, all of us – married or single – will have less cause for fretting and introspection.

Although I've never visited a convent or a monastery, there's no way you'll convince me that those nuns and monks who devote themselves to prayer and meditation and to a life of celibacy are in any way less fulfilled than the mum and dad with three kids around the corner. They're less 'usual', that's for sure, and an easy butt for the world's cynicism, but who's to say that their God-centredness and their single status make them any less than whole people?

Some of the most magnificent and impressive people whose lives have crossed mine have been single missionaries, beavering away in some outlandish bush school or hospital, in response to and in gratitude for the love they receive from God. There's never a trace of bitterness or regret, not a hint of anger or resentment, just not enough minutes in the day to contemplate an alternative family lifestyle.

And so to the second F in my personal reasons for contentment: *freedom*. I recognise that single people can lean towards the selfish. After all, they plan their lives for themselves, there's no wife/husband or children to include in decision-making, and life revolves around one rather than the family.

If I fancy a steak, then that's what I'll have. If I prefer an ITV play to a BBC news programme, I'll switch across without consultation. If I feel like an evening out, there's no one to be left behind and to get upset. That's a pattern of thinking that's surely inevitable for the single person, and I have to own up and say it would be difficult for me to change now. And, to be honest, I really don't want to.

Whereas marriage surely provides freedom in certain areas, it's equally true that it curtails it in others. It's hard, and mostly pointless, to theorise about what might have been, but I can't help wondering how my career would have turned out if I'd married. It would have been different, that's for sure, and may well have ended years ago. Even as I plan this chapter, I'm getting ready for what amounts to six months of touring with virtually no break. Now how could I contemplate that with a wife and children to consider? There's no way I could drag them around with me. But if I'm to sustain a career that sort of planning is crucial. If I opt out and stay at home, my public profile declines, and record sales and audiences dwindle.

People often quiz me about my longevity in the business. How have I outlasted so many others who've made their fleeting mark and then vanished? At least part of the answer is that I've worked at it. Worked consistently and with discipline and with enthusiasm. OK, six months on the road isn't typical, but I'm away from home more often than not, and if I wasn't travelling I'd be immersed in recording or rehearsing or performing. That's both time-consuming and demanding. I honestly don't know whether I could have managed a family lifestyle. Even if my wife and children had coped with me being away for long stretches at a time, I don't think it would have been acceptable to me. As I've said already, if I undertake something I want to do it well and achieve the best possible result. It would be the same with marriage. I'd need to give it everything – total commitment. Anything less makes marriage a nonsense.

But the truth is that never in my life have I had a relationship which asked that much of me, and somehow I don't think I ever shall. It isn't that being a rock star and being married are mutually exclusive. They're not. But if I had a wife, she'd reasonably want a husband first and foremost, and, after a thirty year career, I think I'd find that transition very difficult, if not impossible, to make. The fact is that I enjoy the freedom to figure out for myself how best to spend my time, and the thought of losing that freedom, or even having to adjust it, isn't appealing.

Forgive me, ladies, if that sounds male chauvinist in the extreme. I've already earned myself a five-star rebuke from my secretary. Don't I realise, she says, that marriage is equally disrupting and demanding for the woman? Well, yes, I do, but that doesn't help any. The fact is, loath as I am to admit it, you tend to get a trifle set in your ways by the time the half-century looms, and lifestyle patterns are well and truly established. The fact that my partner would be suffering the same adjustment problem is no great comfort!

A women's magazine, in yet another article revealing 'the truth about why Cliff's never married', decided in its wisdom that it was my 'fear of commitment' rather than 'not having found the right girl'. They were close but not right. It isn't that I fear commitment, rather that I've never felt inclined to make it.

And so to what seems to me to be a real crunch issue for single people, male or female. Freedom from family commitments has to mean freedom to undertake responsibility elsewhere, and although as I've said I find it difficult to relate to the problems of many single people, I bet that more often than not trouble stems from there being a commitment vacuum.

Freedom from family ties to do nothing in particular has to be a disaster, a sure recipe for loneliness and frustration. It may be going over the top a bit to suggest that being single is a privilege, but, in the sense of it allowing the opportunity to be more dedicated to a career and, in my instance, to be involved more practically in my Christian faith, it is.

I wonder just how many great things, or even just plain useful and worthwhile things, have been achieved down the ages by single people for no other reason than that they have been free of domestic ties. Again, I know the missionary scene may be an extreme example, but even in my limited travels to places like Haiti and Sudan I've been amazed by the fantastic caring and devoted work carried out by single women. Presumably if they had married, they'd be at home in Britain or in the States, and I can't help thinking that the world would be the poorer. Similarly, a whole chunk of voluntary and charity work at home is carried out by single people, not because they've nothing better to do, as some jaded cynics have been known to remark, but because they're usually the best equipped and most highly motivated to do it.

Again, don't misunderstand me – I'm not advocating a single existence, I'm one of the most weepy-eyed romantics around. But those of us who are single, for whatever reason, ought to leap at the advantages of giving the world, or one tiny segment of it, the benefit of our commitment. We have more of it to offer!

Of course the bottom line of all this is that, as far as I'm concerned, God is in control of my life and has a purpose for it which may or may not include marriage. That doesn't mean I'm a fatalist. Nor is it a cop-out. It puts the onus on me to discern what his will is and to do it. Sometimes that's difficult, and events aren't always easy to understand or accept, but to be sure deep down that life isn't just a matter of random chance and that there is a plan designed by Someone who wants the absolute best for you enables me at least to relax and to be at peace about things. It's just a shame that others can't share the same perspective.

But, in addition to fulfilment and freedom, there's one other vital component which helps keep the antidepressants at bay, and that's plain old-fashioned *friendship*. There's so much talk about husbands and wives, lovers and live-in partners, and who's going with whom, that mere friends seem to be of little significance in the relationship stakes. Perhaps it's simply that friends are taken for granted or overlooked. What I find really sad and quite a reflection of our times is when the term 'good friends' is devalued with sarcastic 'nudge, nudge, wink, wink' insinuations.

Personally, I believe we underestimate the importance of strong friendship, and I know some people who would be almost embarrassed to refer to someone as 'a good friend'.

Society, they feel, is bound to read more into it than meets the eye. I may be wrong, but I have a feeling that there's a tendency to steer away from developing deep, lasting and uncomplicated friendships. If that's true, we're the poorer for it.

I remember seeing a newsreel shot of an old couple who were celebrating sixty years of married life. When the reporter asked them how they'd stuck each other for so long, the old lady reached over and touched her husband's hand. 'I like him,' she said. And that summed it all up. Whatever else that couple had going for them over the years, friendship was the bedrock of their relationship.

I wish we had a term for friendship equivalent to 'falling in love'. 'Falling in like' somehow isn't quite right! I wonder whether couples who marry and say they're 'madly in love' are necessarily the best of friends as well. I guess it's not always the case, and when the passion dies down and there's no foundation of friendship underneath, then I wonder what's left to make the partnership work.

I have friends, male and female, whom I love – not in the physical, romantic sense, but with great affection, and certainly with deep trust. Those friends, and of course I mean only a handful, account for, along with my mother and sisters, nieces and nephews, the most important human relationships I have, and I can't imagine surviving intact without them. They're people who will tell me when I'm wrong, encourage me when I'm right, and be there when I need them. They're people for whom I have enormous respect, and they're the reason I don't fear a lonely old age, because hopefully they'll still be around to share it with me.

Perhaps it's time we singles started a campaign to foster honest-to-goodness friendships and a climate where the phrase 'just good friends' means exactly what it says, no more and no less.

Finally, perhaps it's the prerogative of married folk to assume that all middle-aged single people are a mass of frustrations and hang-ups, and are eaten up with envy of their married friends. Sorry, but it's a myth! For me, today is just how I want it. Tomorrow, who knows? I'm no crystal ball gazer, and I'm open to whatever God has in store. Meanwhile, I've registered one nugget of advice from a married friend. The acid test, if ever I do consider marriage, should not be, 'Can I imagine being with this girl for ever?', but rather: 'Could I possibly imagine living without her?' Until I get a 'no' to that question, I'll go on enjoying the single life – happily fulfilled, making the most of the freedom, and appreciating great friends.

7 NOW AND THEN

7 NOW AND THEN

Years ago it was 'flower power' – the age of pot, beads and the Maharishi. Most of us watched the antics of 'the Beautiful People' with tolerant amusement, but today there's a new energy sweeping the country, and this time, folks, you'd better believe it! The oldies have come of age, and 'grey power' reigns!

Before you decide I'm barmy, just consider this. According to the *Tatler* magazine, which I can't pretend to read very often, 'the teens, with cash in their pockets, are fast turning into index-linked pensioners. Twenty years more and they will be the only market force to reckon with.'

OK, that may still leave you none the wiser, but for this ever-so-slightly-ageing rocker it's beat to the ears. What it means is that the teeny-boppers who, not so long ago, were the record industry's primary target, and who understandably weren't too keen on buying records by someone old enough to be their grandad, have now grown up, and their replacement generation is a much smaller group. In other words, the population is getting older and majority tastes have changed.

If you think about it, there really has been a shift of emphasis in the last few years. Of course the nine-to-fourteen market is still important and always will be, but it's no longer the be-all and end-all of our industry. How many specifically teeny-bop idols can you name, either bands or individual artists? Not many, I bet. And today our record scene must have an unprecedented array of 'grey power' talent which, if not dominating the charts, seems to have secured a prominent and influential place in them. Elton John, David Bowie, Mick Jagger, Paul McCartney, Rod Stewart, Pink Floyd, Status Quo, Dire Straits, Freddie Mercury – the list of older statesmen is endless. And what's significant is that there's no pressure on us to give up. As far as age is concerned, there's no cut-off point. Just because we don't necessarily appeal to ten-year-old *Tiffany* fans doesn't mean a light – we can still sell a million records to people who are between thirty and sixty, and that's a new and increasingly influential market force.

The challenge to the record companies is to gear themselves to a more discerning and adult audience, and that, I have to say, suits me just fine. At Copenhagen Airport recently, a guy of about fifty came up and asked if I was Cliff Richard. I owned up, and rather sheepishly he said he used to be a fan. As I signed his cigarette packet, he enquired whether I still made records.

After my blood pressure returned to normal I realised that I should in fact have been delighted. For here was evidence again of a huge potential untapped market out there – people of my generation, dormant fans even, who were willing and able to buy product but who just weren't receiving any record company signals. They weren't avid followers of the pop charts and they weren't comfortable browsing through the High Street record shops, which are often 'no-go areas' for anyone over twenty-one!

Somehow the companies must adopt a new style of promotion to get through successfully to those who can retire early and enjoy their wealth. Over the coming years I believe we'll see it.

I suppose it's because I've attained fairly senior 'grey power' status myself that I'm more and more often asked to look back and pontificate about trends and standards in the music business. 'What was it like in your day?' they ask. At which I bite my lip and point out that this *is* my day! And I firmly believe it is. Yesterday and the day before weren't the 'good old days', because today is better. Apart from which, I rarely have the luxury to dwell on the past or wallow in nostalgia, because the present is always so darned busy – and for that I'm grateful.

Nevertheless, while I'm one of the music business's biggest cheerleaders, not all that's happened over the years has been for the better, and not all comparisons between today's disco-orientated scene and the beginning of rock 'n' roll in the late Fifties are favourable. For starters, answer me this: Why is it that whenever you hear a nostalgic medley of classic rock songs there's rarely anything representing the past twenty-five years? Always it's pre-Beatles – 'Good Golly Miss Molly', 'Tutti Frutti', 'Jailhouse Rock', 'Heartbreak Hotel', 'That'll Be The Day', 'Lucille', and dozens more immediately familiar and seemingly ageless melodies are automatic first choice. Why is that there's rarely a Beatles number? Why nothing from the Rolling Stones or The Who? Where's a Dylan or even a Springsteen song? My father and his father before him would say, 'They don't write 'em like they used to.' I say, 'They *can* write 'em – they just don't!'

It isn't that songs were better in the late Fifties or early Sixties, for who's to say what's good and bad in something as subjective as musical taste? But apply the lifespan test and there can't be much room for argument. How many of this year's crop of hits, for instance, will still be performed in twenty or thirty years' time? Of course there are good records produced today – and occasionally some great ones – but I can't help thinking that in the year 2000, when they present the best of the century's rock 'n' roll, it won't be today's material that's selected, but 'Lucille', 'Tutti Frutti', and so on, and so on.

I've already had a swipe at the quality of modern songs in an earlier chapter, but I have to come back to it. Perhaps it's wrong and unfair to bad-mouth song-writing quality. Maybe it isn't that the quality has declined, but rather that styles have changed and become more transient.

The Fifties and early Sixties were very much the era of the three-minute song. I remember meeting Robert Plant at the wedding of a mutual friend and he was kind enough to say that he envied my career, in that I could go out on stage and do a complete, uninterrupted performance. Led Zeppelin at the time were very much into ten- and fifteen-minute musical sagas, and apparently the pattern was for Robert to sing his little segment, return backstage for ten minutes for a cup of tea or something stronger, and only return on stage when the guitarist and bass player had finished their instrumental thrash. 'There are moments', he said, 'when I'd love to go back to a straightforward three-minute song which has a beginning, middle and end!'

I may have missed one, but I can't think of a single song from Elvis, Buddy Holly, Little Richard or Jerry Lee Lewis that lasted more than three to three-and-a-half minutes, and which hasn't stood the test of time. By no stretch of the imagination were the lyrics profound. 'Be Bop A Lula . . .' isn't likely to inspire any great community achievement!

95

But for sheer vitality and enjoyment the songs of that era are unsurpassed. This was the time when rock 'n' roll was young and fun, a celebration of being alive. Today, much of it is self-indulgent and pompous, and the media and the industry manipulators would have us believe that the genuine article has, by definition, to be accompanied by promiscuous sex, drug abuse and over-the-top aggression.

Now I may have a rotten memory, or just be remarkably naive, but I don't believe the early days of rock 'n' roll were like that at all. I know Elvis died drugged and overweight at forty-two, but remember there were at least ten years from the start of his career when all that came across was a wild abandon to the music. It was fun, exuberant, and somehow innocent, even down to the pelvic wriggle and the pouting lip. Sexy maybe – but no way threatening.

Perhaps I can best describe the difference by saying that in those early days the record industry brought out song after song. Today it's a matter of record after record. Many of them sound fabulous. Few of them are great songs, and even fewer will be remembered next year, let alone ten years hence. Exciting and rhythmic sounds may be great to dance to, but if it's at the expense of melody then the end result is a short-lived, quickly dispensable and instantly forgettable factory-line product. And I think that's a shame, because I don't believe it's necessary to compromise on the song simply to get the sound. In my book, the two can and should be compatible, and there are sufficient illustrations from recent charts to prove my point. I'd like to think that some of my material would be among them – titles like 'Miss You Nights', 'Devil Woman' and 'Some People' are going to be around for a long long time, simply because they're class songs.

I also wonder whether vocalists realise that they too are victims in the struggle for the latest 'sound'. Perhaps they're willing victims – I don't know – but so many seem to have sacrificed a really distinctive vocal on the altar of the overall sound.

Again, compare the voices of Elvis, the Everlys, Ricky Nelson, Sam Cook, Jerry Lee Lewis, etc., and you'll see what I mean. They're distinctive, each one part of the rock 'n' roll world, yet absolutely different and able to capture the ear of successive generations of record buyers.

Now how many lead vocalists of today's bands could you

say with any conviction would do the same? There are of course exceptions that prove the rule. Paul Young, Boy George and George Michael all have great voices, and I'm sure they'll be remembered. But, with the best will in the world, I can't imagine the majority of today's chart vocals making the slightest impression on pop history. Perhaps, as I say, they acknowledge and accept that, and a mere contribution to an overall 'feel' is all they intend. If that's so, then good luck to them, and I hope they're satisfied with a career that will last only as long as their particular style is in vogue.

Maybe, on second thoughts, they will have a place in pop history, not as individual artists, but as participants in an era of extraordinary technical advance, and perhaps the absence of emotion and soul merely reflects the times we live in.

Experts have probably done advanced calculations already, but I'm intrigued to know whether there are unlimited variations of melody possible from our little eight-note octave. Could it be that the permutations are wearing a wee bit thin? After all, it's said that Shakespeare wrote the seven definitive plots, and every play since has been a variation on his themes. Goodness knows how many plays have been written over the centuries, but they would be far exceeded by musical scores, all based on just eight notes. It's amazing to think there must be millions of combinations, but can it actually go on for ever? It's mathematically beyond me!

Certainly you'd never suspect any diminishing reserves if weekly record output is anything to go by. At peak times of the year, particularly during the run-up to Christmas, it has been known for as many as eight hundred releases to flood the market in one week. That's exceptional, but the average has to be way over a hundred. Now personally I don't think that's necessarily a bad thing. I'm a great believer in choice and an element of competition, and the fact that a hundred artists are struggling each week to achieve the playlist and a relative handful of available chart positions is healthy for them and healthy for me. As each year progresses, so the battle gets harder. At around the fifty mark you're fighting all the odds – the fashion, the hype, and the assumption (a totally wrong one, as I've shown) that rock 'n' roll is for youngsters. It amazes and galls a lot of the music press that occasionally I'm still able to beat those odds.

But competition, as I say, isn't simply about age. Today music is much more complex, and there's no question that bands who come through now are far more musically talented and equipped than the Shadows and I were when we first started. Our early stuff was all based around three, four or five chords, and today's musical know-how would have left us standing. Despite that, it's satisfying to know that we contributed a little to the musical foundations on which successive bands have built. Even before the Beatles, we were putting down a permanent plank or two.

Like everything else, competition has its bad effects as well, and in the scrummage to get our noses in front of the next guy there has emerged a sort of professional one-upmanship. This band tours with an entourage of fifty people. Wow – they must be terrific! That band uses eight hundred white lights in their rig. Now they have to be something incredible! Of course it doesn't follow, but it's a vicious circle, all desperately trivial, yet at the same time a hard spiral to avoid.

It's all speculation of course, and it's dangerous to generalise, but I'm not sure whether it wasn't a whole lot tougher for a successful band twenty or thirty years ago than it is now. Even after the Shadows and I had hit records, we still used to rattle around the country in a Bedford boneshaker and stay at those infamous bed and breakfast guesthouses. That was the routine for at least two years. Today, failing air travel, there are luxury sleeper coaches kitted out with video and computer games, and accommodation is in the local Holiday Inn or Trust House Forte. Maybe a bit of 'roughing it' was good for the soul, but give me today's comforts any time.

People talk more these days about the pressures and strains of show business, but again I'm not convinced they're any greater than they ever were, and whether you're competing against a hundred or ten others for a chart position the principle's the same. Artists are sensitive, vulnerable people – we always have been and always will be – and when our art is criticised and put down we get hurt. That's the pressure, and basically nothing's new. But I can find little sympathy for those who huff and puff about the trials and strains of hard work. At least we're doing the very thing we most want to do, and that is to make music. If that's a pressure, we shouldn't be doing it in the first place.

I need some convincing, too, that it takes a year and a half plus a million pounds to make a good album. Just occasionally there's an exceptional album that reflects that level of investment, but it's rare. And I hate to think how many millions have been totally and utterly wasted by bands whose studio self-indulgence is really ridiculous.

I grind my teeth even more when we're conned into believing that interminable remixing and astronomical costs guarantee exceptional quality. That's a rubbish equation, and over the years too many record company executives have fallen for it. Hopefully, though, perhaps the days of pampering undisciplined and spoilt artists are over, and I seem to detect a much more workmanlike approach generally to recording costs and schedules. I guess, as always, the bottom line eventually has the last word!

What I think has changed radically over the years is the diminishing of what I call 'star aura'. For many that will seem a good thing, but personally I regret it. Charisma, star image, call it what you like, but among the younger crowd there ain't much of it about!

I've been saying for a number of years that we seem to be heading into an age of normality. We don't have megastars any more, at least no new ones. Most of the kids in the street can actually sing like their favourite recording artists, and it wasn't like that a while back. Much as I wanted to, I couldn't sing like Elvis, and I still can't. When I became a fan of Jerry Lee Lewis and Little Richard, the best I could do was a poor copy. I could sing in my own way, but I couldn't reproduce their special sound.

These days, if you go to a disco and hear people sing along with the records, they sound genuinely similar to the vocals on vinyl (minus the echo), and to me that's amazing. Today the whole trend, both in singing and in image, is towards the ordinary – to look the same, sound the same, and often behave the same as the guy in the street – and for me that robs the industry of a lot of its excitement and mystique.

Sure, in ordinary life I'm no different to anyone else, and certainly no better, but on stage it's a different world, and I'll pull every trick in the book to look different, sound different and be different, in order to express that piece of fantasy which I believe is exactly what the audience wants and pays for. They ask to be wafted away into another realm, and how can that even begin to happen if on stage I'm the spitting image of the bloke next door?

For me, performing is about creating illusions, and I can't do that standing in my socks, with greasy hair, spots on my nose, and tatty jeans. Admittedly, it's up to all artists to create their own audience rapport, but for me the sort of familiarity which makes you just 'their mate up there' would never work. And if, as I've heard my fans say on occasions, I'm personally inaccessible, then that's just how I plan it. But don't misunderstand me – for virtually every night for a year during *Time* I stopped behind after the show to sign stage-door autographs. Being separate doesn't mean being aloof.

It follows, I suppose, that, if I'm in favour of image-building, I can hardly be critical of what's generally called record hype. And, to be honest, I lean towards accepting it as par for the course. While I draw the line at exploiting the financial vulnerability of kids, I can only smile at all that nonsense concocted about the Beastie Boys, for instance, when I know there were a few exaggerated claims, to say the least, about me in the early days. Mind you, the time I do get peeved is when a hyped band or artist takes up a precious position in the charts. That's frustration in the extreme, especially if I'm in the slot just below!

The Americans were of course masters of hype, and, thinking back, there's little doubt that people like Frankie Avalon and Fabian were totally contrived artists. Fabian, it's said, was spotted by a record man as he drove along the street, and was signed up virtually on the pavement, purely on the strength of his good looks. Fabian protested that he couldn't sing a note, but he was more than happy to be packaged and hyped as the archetypical hunky American man. Sure enough, in the States it worked and Fabian became a monster star. Over here, he remained relatively unknown, because we got the record without the hype, and without that there was little to shout about!

The point is that when product depends on hype for its success there's a hefty question mark over the staying-power of the artist concerned. Believe me, people don't last in our business if they're without talent. The public can be fooled by the promotion men once or even twice, but they're far too discerning to be taken in permanently.

The Beastie Boys are a classic example of a promotion man's skill. When I started this book, they were splashed across every national tabloid. If you believed what you read, they seemed to be threatening the very stability of the country. Yet the whole thing was absolute eyewash. The Beastie Boys weren't unusual, they weren't even ugly! Today, as the book is nearly through, I don't hear a whisper about them. Could it be that they've vanished from the scene as suddenly as they arrived? If so, the worst that happened was that thousands of impressionable kids wasted a few pounds, while the band's record company laughed all the way to the bank. What it seems the Beastie Boys didn't have was the benefit of a caring and wise record chief to advise them and steer them on their way.

And that reflects another unfortunate change. Today, many companies are satisfied with their 'fashion-orientated' policy, and there isn't the emphasis on or investment in building careers which last. Gone, it seems, are the Norrie Paramors of the record companies, the A & R guys whose job it was to nurture their young artists, to egg them on and mould their careers. Now, the priority criterion is who looks right for the day. And when the day's out, why worry? There's always plenty more to choose from for tomorrow.

An executive at one major company told me just a few weeks back that their artists' roster includes only one 'new generation' band that seems to have any chance of lasting. The rest, he predicted, would be forgotten within three to five years, perhaps less.

U2's Bono made me sit up and think with that comment of his that rock 'n' roll is 'the soundtrack to change'. Now I've yet to meet Bono, and I'm sure that when I do I'll understand his attitude and thinking more clearly, but again I wonder whether we're in danger of elevating rock 'n' roll to a higher and more important plane than it really deserves.

I mentioned earlier that when I started lyrics were certainly lightweight, to put it kindly. 'Don't step on my blue suede shoes' was considered pretty aggressive stuff, while 'Bachelor Boy' was about as near as anyone got to social comment! It was Bob Dylan who, in the very early Sixties first began to use his music for serious statement and sincere protest – although I was among the many, I suspect, who understood and appreciated Dylan's poetry much better when it was spoken rather than sung. Rock 'n' roll nevertheless became infused with a message: 'The world needs changing,' said Dylan, 'and the new generation is going to change it.' For the first time, commercial pop moved on from 'Peggy Sue' and 'Living Doll', and Dylan's lyrics effectively touched many raw nerves around the world.

And then came the Beatles, with allegedly message-laden songs which people took so seriously that profound meanings were discovered where none were intended. As far as I'm concerned, much as I admire the Beatles' music, any message there may have been died with John Lennon, and in truth I suspect that Paul, George and Ringo must sometimes chuckle up their sleeves at the pretentious analysis of their work that's occasionally trotted out by various 'erudite' pop historians. I think it was Paul who once admitted that many Beatles' songs were inspired by a current newspaper headline, rather than by any burning philosophy which the guys felt compelled to get across.

In the years since, rock 'n' roll has been used to reflect a whole spectrum of attitudes and political outlooks. *Live Aid* saw the rock industry join forces – and some force it was too – to cry on behalf of the world's poor. And, in the run-up to the last general election, we saw rock bands, usually of a leftish persuasion, publicly canvassing for votes from their concert stage.

And then there's me. For twenty years at least I've had no qualms at all about injecting Christian values and themes into much of my material, even though I can't escape the impression that of all messages – political, philosophical, or whatever – it's the one that raises most hackles and obstruction. But that's another story.

So you might think I'd be at one with Bono about the social importance of rock 'n' roll. In fact I'm not so sure that I am, particularly if he believes that the music itself is the message. Having done my own concerts as a Christian through two decades now, I'm convinced that the spoken word is infinitely more powerful than the sung lyric when it comes to conveying some important truth. Bono's right – there *is* a power in rock music, but it's terribly limited, and personally I don't believe that in itself its influence is as great as some people in the industry would claim.

It may seem an odd opinion for a professional singer, but I'm sure that what counts in terms of influence isn't so much what we sing and perform, but how we live and what we say, both on stage and off. They are the areas of genuine lasting influence. That doesn't mean I shall stop singing songs that reflect my faith. If I can find material good enough, I'll still use it. But if I'm genuinely concerned at all about getting the message across, it's my life and words that will prove the real communication. Rock 'n' roll can only go so far, and we'd do well to keep it in perspective. Artists and bands with a message, whatever it might be, must discover, as I did, that the music is of little consequence apart from a compatible lifestyle.

So what of the future? I'm not too hot about interpreting or predicting trends, but the frequency with which some 'golden oldie' pops up in the charts, either re-vamped or in original pristine condition, makes me think or hope that all is not lost when it comes to song appreciation. It may be that so much apparently ageless material will inspire the new guys to learn a lesson from yesterday's writers and start considering goose-bumps on the arms, as well as bass drums in the disco. And, no, that doesn't mean we'll be putting the clock back. Rock 'n' roll will always forge ahead and find new forms and outlets, and today it's as alive and vibrant as ever it was.

What I do know is that technically we are moving near to recording perfection. We can't be far from it already, with our amazing digital techniques. Although, strangely enough, having recorded my voice digitally in a recent studio session, I felt we lost something, and reverted to the old faithful analogue method – straight on to tape. Some-how we found we could do more with the voice in terms of EQ-ing than we could digitally, but maybe that was just a quirk of my voice on the day, and I certainly have nothing but awed respect for the guys who have developed studio recording into an exciting and challenging science.

As for me, I view the prospect of another thirty years in the industry with a kind of mischievous relish. The thought of Cliff Richard still having hits well into the twenty-first century may cause dismay and suicidal tendencies for some, but you'd better face it, it could well happen. For, despite all the hype and the crass awfulness of some of the music business's output, and although at times people who should know better act irresponsibly and greedily, I still love what I do and what I'm part of.

Every profession has its shortcomings, and the music business is no exception, but it's given me thirty years of incredible satisfaction and enjoyment, so despite my criticisms (which I think I've earned the right to express) my heart is as much in it now as it ever was. Years ago there may have been something almost obscene about a middle-aged singer performing rock 'n' roll, but today there's no apology necessary or called for. It was my generation who grew up having invented rock 'n' roll, and, what's more, we still know how to do it!

8 GOING PLACES

8 GOING PLACES

I guess I'm just easily pleased. Either that, or I'm the worst kind of Philistine slob when it comes to travel opportunities and appreciating the exotic wonders of the world. The fact is I enjoy being at home, and overseas tours and get-away holidays are only good value if the sun shines hot and long, and if tennis courts nestle no more than a lob away from hotel apartments.

I must be the only tourist who chose to fry in the Israeli sun beside the Dead Sea, rather than scale the apparently remarkable battlements of Masada, where hundreds committed suicide back in early Jewish history.

And what idiot would go all the way to Miami, Florida, to turn his back on Disneyworld for an hour with the hotel tennis pro?

And I hardly dare mention my one and only visit to Moscow, when a particularly dreary hotel bedroom seemed a better option than a peek at Lenin's Tomb! I'm not proud of my lack of cultural appetite. It's the way I am, and history and architectural relics have never exactly zapped me with inspiration.

Not so with natural beauty, and before I self-inflict too good a hatchet job, I'm proud to say that one of my five all-time favourite places is a remote little village in North Wales where, in the early Seventies, I bought a package of land and a tiny cottage with three foot thick stone walls and the biggest open hearth you've ever seen.

I think it has to be one of the most ruggedly beautiful areas on earth and, although it rains buckets and somehow a tennis court would seem a greedy intrusion, for me it's probably the most therapeutic of all oases. Just occasionally – and sadly it isn't nearly as often as I'd like – I pack the car with a few tins, sturdy wellies, sweaters, anorak, and the guitar, perch the dog on the top and take off for what's inevitably a five-hour-plus journey. That's why I make it so seldom. It's rare for me to have five days clear of commitments, and a weekend just isn't enough time to get over the drive and unwind.

But, I tell you, that place is a treat. Somehow it's possible to duck out from all the pressures and activity and just be still. Even if it's lashing down with rain outside, the sense of security and well-being within that little hillside cottage is immense, and I know nowhere like it for simply mar- shalling my thoughts and checking priorities. I know, for instance, I can pray more readily in Wales, not just because there is little else to do except walk and sleep, but because the whole place shrieks out about the reality of a Creator. The hills and mountains, the waterfalls and streams, different and seemingly more breathtaking views around each successive corner, remind me constantly of David's reaction in the Psalms: 'When I consider . . . the work of your fingers . . . what is man that you are mindful of him?'

And somehow the rain doesn't seem quite as wet in Wales. It's even exhilarating, and many's the time I've driven to Conway Bay and walked along the beach there in hard driving rain. With woolly socks, gum-boots, and anorak hard down over the head, it doesn't really matter how sodden an apparition you look. In Wales no one cares two hoots, and a long hot bath, a spot of home cooking and a curl-up in front of the fire, watching TV, isn't too far away from paradise. Whether the dog, exhausted, bedraggled and frustrated by thousands of infuriating sheep, would agree is another matter.

A few friends find it surprising that I should take off to Wales on my own. They seem to think I should find it lonely 'holed up in the middle of nowhere', as they put it. I'll admit that anything more than a week might get heavy going, but for a few days it's bliss – and it isn't all tinned food either. I'm a dab hand with a leg of lamb, parsnips and roast potatoes, and if it's sauces you like then I'm your man. If record sales fold one day, then work as a sauce chef at a London hotel would suit me just fine.

Quite apart from what the cottage gives me, I also feel a sense of satisfaction that, because the land is used by the Forestry Commission for tree-planting, I have contributed in some small way to oxygenating this planet of ours. In fact it was a Christian conservationist who first enthused me about investing in forestry development land. I owned shares at the time in tin mines in Australia, breweries in New Zealand, or wherever, and had no interest in them whatever. Far better to put money into something generally beneficial, it seemed to me, and over the years we planted out some three or four plots of around 2,500 acres.

It seemed extraordinary to me that the press should have a go at me when I sold the plot – not the cottage, I hasten to add – and they hinted that I'd somehow made a fortune at the taxpayers' expense. Some kind of legal loophole, they called it. They never acknowledged the fact that, at the time of the investment, the government was actually encouraging people like me to direct funds into forestry development, nor did they bother to discover that, according to my business advisers, I never made a penny on the deal anyway. If I'd held on to the land for a few more years, perhaps I would have done, but we decided to put the money elsewhere, so we sold. Not for the first time, the press got it wrong!

What's more seriously disheartening is that the equivalent of all the wood that was grown on my land, over my years of ownership, is regularly chopped down in a matter of minutes in places like the Amazon, resulting in barren land, shortage of rainfall, food deficiency, and so on. I wonder if we'll ever learn.

But back to the cottage, and I admit it has crossed my mind that one day I might hear that the Welsh Nationalists have set the place alight as part of their protest against absentee English landlords. Maybe the fact that a local family has its home in one part of the L-shaped cottage has kept me out of their line of fire! Let's hope it stays that way. Any damage done to that little hideaway would be a tragedy.

While I can't pretend to be involved with local village life and have mastered the Welsh language only to the extent of being able to pronounce – not spell! – 'norsta, cariad' and 'cabana da dwr' (which, roughly interpreted, is 'Goodnight, darling' and 'Have a cup of tea'), I sense only warmth and welcome from the locals, some of whom have never ventured beyond their fields of sheep, let alone the next village!

At first they were perhaps a bit cagey, and I can well imagine that a pop singer from London wouldn't be their first choice of immigrant, but the 'fishing rights' changed all that. One of my boundaries is a fabulous fast-flowing river, packed with trout and salmon. Five or six hundred yards of riverbank with fishing rights was the key to establishing good relationships. Forget the cottage and the hundreds of acres of forest and grazing land. What would I do with a muddy strip of riverbank?

It was the butcher who picked the short straw on behalf of the villagers. Would I consider selling the fishing rights, for a nominal cost, you understand, to the local old folk, who loved their bit of angling? How could I refuse? I kept the rights to just one line for any enthusiastic fisherman who uses the cottage, and the others are now enjoyed by Jones the Post, Evans the Bread, and all the rest.

I do have one other holiday home and, to be honest, it's a bit more palatial than the Welsh cottage. It's what the estate agents, I think, would describe as 'a des. res.'. I've had a kind of love affair with Portugal ever since Peter Gormley, my now-retired manager, bought property there back in the early Sixties. In fact it was TV presenter and producer, Mu Young, who raved to Peter about this little-known area called the Algarve which was so great for holidays, easy to get to even in those days, and fantastic for investment. Well, she was right on all counts, and although now I have a different property there than the original one, to my mind there's nowhere else within reasonable striking distance of Britain that can provide the same charm, character and guaranteed sunshine. A few million other Europeans have made the same discovery over the last few years, as it happens, but somehow the place has kept its essential character and feel.

For the most part, the extensive tourist development has been controlled wisely, and even the cheapest and smallest of new villas and apartments are thoughtfully designed to blend with the older Moorish-style buildings. Although there are the occasional loud-mouthed, pink-shouldered Brits who shout after me in the village square and make me cringe, I love the peace and beauty of my clifftop villa, where I can bask in the sun and do absolutely nothing, other than listen to music, read a book, and flop into the pool when it all gets too exhausting. In fact, if the strain of lying down gets too unbearable, there's a tennis court to ensure I don't seize up completely.

Somehow the Algarve area seems to absorb two kinds of

tourists: the ones like me, who want their privacy, and the others for whom a holiday would be a disaster without nightly discos, sardine-packed beaches, and something resembling an English pub within easy staggering distance. I guess it takes all sorts!

Not for me, by the way, those white and sandy beaches. Lovely to look at and to photograph, invigorating to walk along, but ghastly to stick to with a tacky layer of sunshine oil!

What the locals make of this annual summer invasion, I can't imagine. Of course many of them take full advantage of it and, from May till September, earn a relative fortune from letting their homes, running restaurants and working in hotels. Yet, for the majority – on the surface at least – it seems as though they are largely oblivious to the hordes who disrupt their simple lifestyle. The fishermen, the farmers and the orange-growers go about their work as they've always done, and the little wizened black-clad women, all of whom look at least a hundred and ten, munch on their gums in the shade of the fig trees, apparently ignoring the outside world that has come to play.

Yet even for these old dears I suspect that life isn't quite the same. I'll never forget the sweet lady who turned up to buy my original house – quite a large imposing place, virtually in the middle of town. There must be a misunderstanding, I thought, as this bent old body creaked up the steps. Not a bit of it. In she came, plonked her thread-bare shopping bag on the table, and began to count out the thousands in crisp new notes. The last time I saw her she was living in the garage among piles of washing and crates of lemonade, and had let the house for nine months of the year. Sometimes that which doesn't glitter must have a very golden touch!

I suppose it's something to do with familiarity and the fact that it's only a two-and-a-half hour flight away, but, despite holidays in the Caribbean, Florida and other exotic places, I always seem to gravitate back to the Algarve. Maybe it's the sunsets, the donkey carts or the fig farms, or the excitement of discovering yet another cheap but wonderful local restaurant. I'm not sure, but whatever it is, I'm sure the Portuguese Tourist Board must owe me a big favour!

Yet, love it as I do, there's one other place in the world, apart from England, where I could imagine myself living, and that's Australia. Hank Marvin and his family have already packed up and joined the huge number of self-exiled Britons in sun-soaked Perth. Before the rumours start, I'd better stress that I have no plans to sell up and follow him. As it is, Australia will have its work cut out coping with Hank. But I can understand why he's gone, and I understand why half of my band are always so unsettled when we come back from a tour there. Basically it's the climate, the lifestyle and the character of the people, and that combination enables a fantastic balance between work and play.

Certainly we never work or play so hard as when we perform in Aussie. Our concerts in the evenings become highlights for us because we've had such great days together beforehand. When you have to perform concerts night after night for six weeks or more, you need something to keep the adrenalin going and to ensure that every show is as important as the opening night. I have to be honest and say that on some tours concerts can be a right drag for everyone. The guys are bored, morale is low, and we can't wait to get home. That's never the case in Australia. Instead of wondering what to do to pass another day, there's just not enough time to play all the tennis, visit all the beaches, eat at all the restaurants, and soak in what I can only describe as a feeling of immense physical freedom.

I remember eating at Doyles, a famous fish restaurant, right by the water's edge on Rose Bay – or was it Watson's Bay? – Sydney. As the lobster thermidor melted in the mouth, half of the group at the next table suddenly got up and plunged into the sea. Back they came ten minutes later, dripping and breathless, to order their second course. No formalities or inhibitions, just healthy outgoing behaviour typical of the Aussie way of doing things.

Incidentally, talking of restaurants – and in case Hank should ever read this – the most fantastic Indian restaurant in the world has to be 'The Shoba' in William Street, Perth. It's worth a dip in the wallet, Hank – if the zip hasn't rusted! Ask for Richard, and say Cliff sent you!

Sydney always seems to me like a city on holiday, and that's where I'd choose to set up home. All those magnificent bays, with stunning views from just about every

For me, my garden is almost as important as the house. I only wish I had shares in our local garden centre!
(Photo: Colin Ramsay)

Dave Clark and I never worked together till TIME even though my sister, Jacqui, ran his fan club back in the sixties. *(Photo: Hanne Jordan)*

As usual, the fans plied me with goodies throughout my 'TIME', and there was plenty of scope for creative cookery. Some of the local hospitals were discharging some very overweight patients!
(Photo: Hanne Jordan)

(Photo: Janet Rainey)

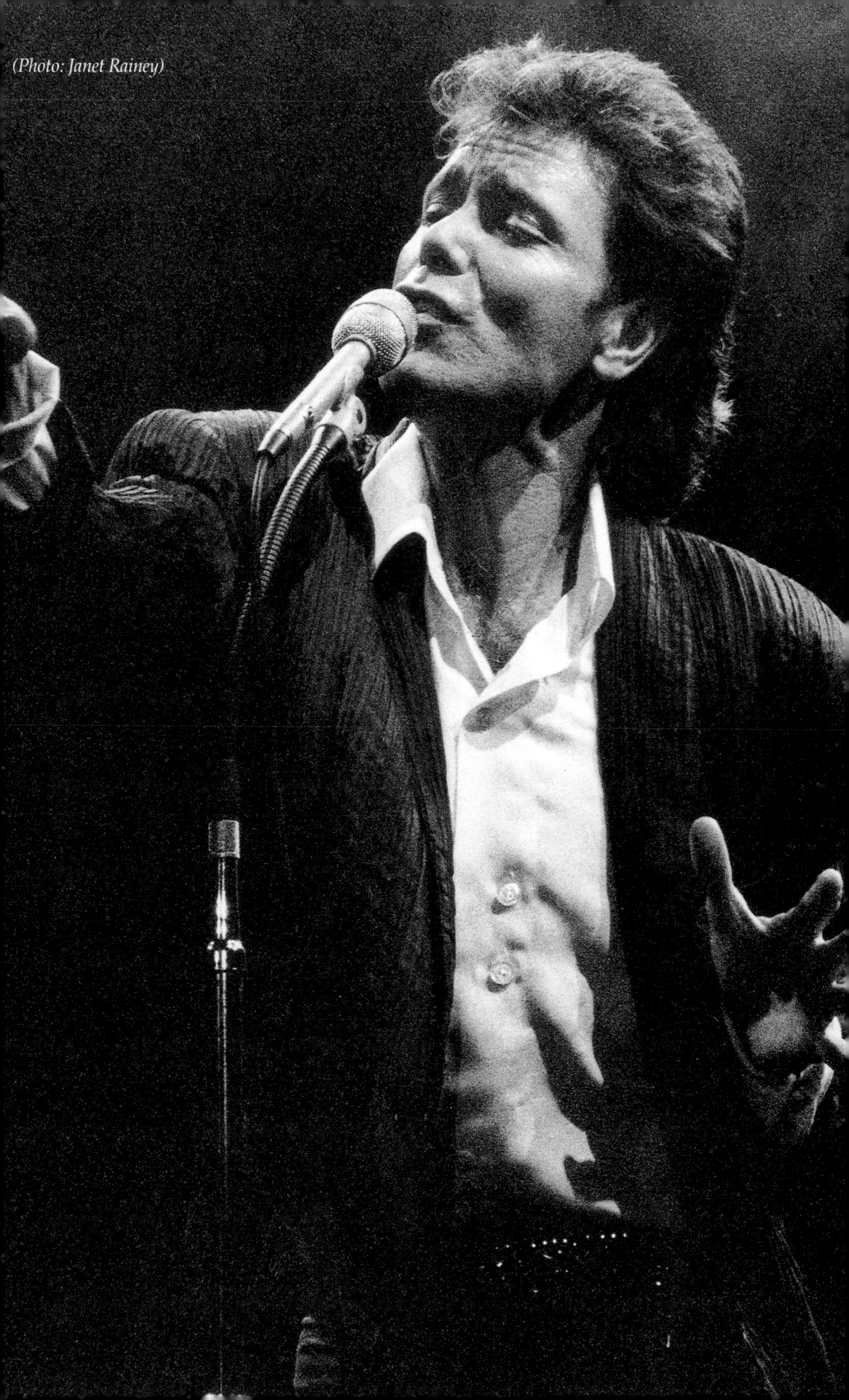

For years now I've been spoiled by regular sell-out concert attendances throughout the UK. In 1987 I was the first artist, apparently, to sell out the 11,500 capacity National Exhibition Centre in Birmingham for six consecutive nights. Just don't let me get complacent, that's all.

(Photo: Hanne Jordan)

I put up with those hair extensions for just as long as it took to establish my character. Hopefully never again! *(Photo: Hanne Jordan)*

We're replacing the statue with this life-size wax effigy.   *(Photo: Colin Ramsay)*

window and doorway, and, although it's a big city, some-how there's a close-knit feel about it. Whatever time of year we tour, I just know that when we stay at the Sebel Townhouse I'll bump into Dire Straits, Billy Connolly, Julio Iglesias, Eric Clapton, or somebody from our industry who just happens to be in town.

I guess that for me half the attraction about Australia is that I have such an enthusiastic following there. My 'Living Doll' with The Young Ones was at Number One for seven weeks, and these days we play concerts at the biggest venues possible. In Darwin, for instance, we played in an amphitheatre which was packed with twelve thousand people. Around three thousand more couldn't get in and, when you think that the population of the whole area is only about sixty thousand, that's not a bad proportion.

It wasn't always like that. In the Seventies we struggled to fill two-thousand seater places, but with the aid of promoter Dennis Smith, who happens to be Dame Edna Everage's manager and had faith in my work and in what the band and I could do, we planned three tours within just five years, and things slowly but surely built up. Today Australia figures regularly in our touring programme, and we know the audiences there almost as well as the British crowd.

In Brisbane, for instance, it's a raucous audience, really wild and supportive, with whoops and whistles to rival the best of American concert-goers. In Sydney, they're warm and responsive, more of a merging of over-the-top Amer-ican and polite British reserve – again, to my mind, a typical reflection of Australia's happy balance between us en-thusiasm without the hype, and British stability without the inhibitions. In short, honestly brash! Going west into Hank territory, you can expect Perth to offer the very best of British!

In many ways South Africa falls into a similar category. And, although it's more fashionable to wipe out that country with a few self-righteous clichés, for me it also ranks among my favourite places. In the main, of course, countries are the people – no more, no less – and in South Africa I have a number of good and very special friends. Mostly they are Christian friends, and that always results in a bond that's somehow closer and more special than others.

113

All my recent visits to South Africa have been for specifically Christian purposes – gospel concerts or church meetings – and I suppose the fact that I felt in some way useful there has produced a particular affection. I know the condemnation that South Africa and its people have received, and it has hurt and disappointed me – not because I feel that the condemnation was unjust, but because it has been delivered so often without love and without compassion for all segments of the community.

A while back there was a cruel song o.. *Spitting Image* which had the refrain, '. . . but I've never met a nice South African'. Well, I have – many of them, of all races – and I feel really offended when the world tars every one of them with the same apartheid brush.

For me, South Africa is where John Perry, one of my former backing vocalists, was converted, and really and truly became a new person. It's where I learnt to waterski, and where I won a tennis tournament and had a custard pie smashed in my face for my efforts; where I've laughed longer and louder than probably anywhere else; and where I've enjoyed the best and deepest of Christian fellowship.

As I write, the future of South Africa and all its people is in the melting-pot. Whether I'll ever go back I don't know, but I'd like to. I'm only grateful for the happy memories it has given me.

Finally, at the risk of sounding too corny, I have to tell you about my favourite of all places to be – and that's home. I always feel there's something badly wrong when people search for every possible excuse to be away from home longer and later. For me, home holds no tensions, no bad vibes, and no risk of boredom. When I drive through the old white gates of the Surrey estate, it's as though the responsibilities and pressures of being Cliff Richard drain away and I can be me. No haloes to keep polished, no image to sustain or live up to. If I want to, I can flop around in slippers and dressing-gown, and there's no one to intrude or make demands.

I suppose it's hard to understand how much a haven home can be if you're not saddled with a famous face. Outside my front door there's no possibility of anonymity or getting lost in a crowd. There's always the expectation to smile, to sign, and to be available. I'm not grumbling, you understand. It's the lifestyle I chose, but if home is where my heart is, it's also where my privacy is, and that's a precious commodity.

Rightly or wrongly, having given a lot to my work and to my fans, I dislike it when either encroaches into my home. Hopefully I'm not too discourteous when fans do call, but I do make it quite clear that this is a taboo area. Once I've signed the autograph, I appreciate the fact that they wave goodbye!

People sometimes ask what I do at home, and the honest answer is 'not much'. I love the garden, and in the summer I potter around and check up that everything is doing what it should. The place is a colourful mass of roses, rhododendrons and azaleas, and Joe, the gardener, does a fantastic job. He's one of those guys who takes enormous pride in his work – something that sadly seems to be increasingly contrary to the spirit of the day.

A while ago we laid some new lawn, and I offered to buy a new sit-on mower to make cutting a bit easier. No thanks, said Joe, he couldn't get the lines as straight!

I like to think I'm reasonably knowledgeable, particularly about trees and shrubs, and I'm an avid listener to *Gardeners' Question-Time* on BBC radio. I'm tempted to phone in one day and ask why the wistaria which we planted at my first Surrey home in the early Seventies, and which would have encased the house in leaves and tentacles every few weeks if we'd let it, gave us, over some fourteen years, the princely total of sixteen blooms. I counted them personally! Answers on a postcard, please.

My immediate home area is well served with garden centres, and I must have spent a fortune on plants and bulbs, half of which have provided nutritious fodder for an assortment of apparently half-starved rabbits, squirrels and foxes – not to mention the fattest and most sluggish pigeons you've ever seen. In fact I've probably spent more making my garden look good than on ornaments and whatever for inside the home. Burglars, please note!

You will have gathered that I don't care to bring work home with me, so the result is that, even though it's only twenty-two miles from London, my home assumes another kind of holiday base. I relax there, and that means walking the dog or watching a video – which I do, flat on the floor, propped up with cushions! It's easier on the back that way, and the chest is really useful for supporting the bowl of

115

tinned guavas, garnished with evaporated milk and a blob of vanilla ice-cream, all liberally sprinkled with grape-nuts – sheer bliss!

Apart from the privacy of it all, I suppose the feeling of security is equally important. Some people, my mum included, say they could never live in a place where you can't see your neighbours. Too isolated, they reckon. Yet I love the isolation, and the neighbours are there if you need them – but, like me, they prefer to enjoy their family privacy from high-powered business lifestyles. The security lies in what is so totally familiar. I once lived in a huge six-bedroomed mansion in Essex, but it was so big there were parts of it we simply never used. My Surrey home is still large by anyone's standards, but, inside at least, it isn't palatial. I haven't lived there long, but everyone who visits says it's warm and feels like home.

It was back in the mid-Sixties that I first shared a house with Bill Latham (who is now one of my management team) and his mother Mamie. Over the years Mamie became very much a second mum to me and shared so much of what I did. She was also gracious and elegant, put up with many strange callers, and coped patiently with all sorts of unpredictable demands and circumstances.

In April 1986 Mamie became very ill and was taken to hospital. I was just a fortnight into my daily stint in *Time*, and on 24 April arrived at the Dominion stage door only to be told that I wasn't needed and could go home. Apparently some machinery had broken down backstage and it would take at least three days to repair. There was no option but to cancel the show.

For many fans, including more than a hundred who had come over from Denmark, it was frustrating and disappointing. But for me it was a godsend. On the evening of Thursday 24 April, when I should have been on stage, I was able to visit the hospital and kiss Mamie goodbye for the last time. She was eighty-four.

'Feather Green' could never be quite the same again, and it was one of the reasons I moved. Something was missing. When I got home late at night, it was strange to see Mamie's bedroom door open. I imagined her sitting in her favourite chair and I still miss her love and her presence.

What I feel must be only a tiny part of Bill's grieving, but I know that for him, as well as for me, there has been a quiet unspoken assurance that we shall experience Mamie's fun and graciousness again. Like many of her generation, she never spoke much about her faith, and I don't remember her ever going to a church service. Somehow it seems hardest to talk about Christian things with the people you are closest to. I've talked my heart out a thousand times across a thousand dinner tables, discussing the claims of Jesus and the relevance of the Christian life, but with Mamie it was so difficult. Perhaps I felt it was unnecessary to go into things too deeply. Perhaps I was kidding myself and didn't want to embarrass her or myself. Yet today, although I regret my reluctance to be more up-front, I am convinced that Mamie had a simple trust in Jesus and believed that he died for her. That was all it needed.

9 BURIED TREASURE

9 BURIED TREASURE

Virtually every night for a year I was put on the spot. 'What', asked Melchisedic in *Time*, 'is the most important thing in your life?'

Hardly the sort of question you'd want to cope with after a heavy day at the office, particularly if your life and the future of Planet Earth depended on it. But, performance after performance, audiences waited on the edge of their seats, chocolates poised between box and mouth, for some deep and memorable insight. A pregnant pause, some pretty convincing (I thought) emotional sobs, and the moment of truth. 'My voice,' I'd blurt out, 'and its right to be heard. No! Wait!' I shrieked before some thunderbolt was unleashed, 'My voice and the *necessity* for it being heard!'

Well, it may have been an anticlimax for the audience, and chocolates certainly resumed their final journey, but it was good enough for Melchisedic. The earth was allowed yet another chance to mend its ways. Personally, if I'd been the Time Lord, I'd have given the earth the chop with no second thoughts on the strength of an answer like that. But then it was only fiction and, although my character's reply wasn't exactly profound, the question has to be one of the most crucial and telling that anyone can ever ask of themselves in real life.

What is most important to me? What do I really value most and can say, with hand on heart, are my top priorities? Is there anything or anybody that I'd put my life on the line for, or is there nothing actually that important?

'Where your treasure is,' says Jesus, 'there your heart will be also.' In other words, our greatest loves or the things we value most reflect the sort of people we are. And that can sometimes be a disturbing discovery.

I had to think very carefully about agreeing to put my name to that massive advertising campaign for the Christian book *Power For Living* early in 1986. Just about every national newspaper and major magazine in the country carried full-page black-and-white, and sometimes colour, advertisements proclaiming under my head-and-shoulders photograph that for Cliff Richard the most important thing in life was not his music or career but his 'personal relationship with God'.

Now, I tell you, it's one thing to declare that from the confines of a pulpit, quite another to see it blazoned across a page of *The Times*! But I knew it was true, so why be coy? I didn't hesitate for long. The opportunity was just too fantastic to pass, and I have to say that I felt that church leaders were slow, both to applaud the American group of Christians who initiated and paid over $1 million for the campaign, and to take full advantage of it and use it as a springboard for other things.

Maybe they thought it was all too good to be true, and to see a whole page commending the Christian faith and the Bible amidst the junk of a daily newspaper somehow didn't register. Maybe Christians jumped to the conclusion that only some cranky cult could have the nerve to advertise in the national press. It's hardly the done thing, after all, more's the pity. If that was the case, I'm sorry they didn't have more confidence in my own discernment between what's cranky and what's true and balanced.

Certainly the American Christians who picked up the tab, as they say over there, were sensible folk who have the responsibility of administering an enormous legacy left by a wealthy Christian businessman. Their brief is to use the fortune to present the claims of Christ to as many people as possible throughout the world, and what more effective way to do it than through newspaper ads and billboards in strategic places, such as the London Underground. If the law had allowed them, they would have added a whole series of TV commercials, but unlike America we don't permit religious bodies of any kind to buy transmission time, and I think that's probably a good thing.

As it was, there were some 300,000 responses to that three-month campaign, and everyone who wrote in received, totally free of charge, a well-written and well-produced book containing the testimonies of a number of Christians, and spelling out the basics of the Christian faith. Of those 300,000, I'm told that around forty thousand wrote again, asking for a follow-up book of Bible studies and indicating a personal spiritual interest. No one was embarrassed or hassled for money, no one came knocking at the door, and no one has been pestered by subsequent mailings. The campaign had total integrity, was a unique form of Christian witness and I felt genuinely privileged to be part of it, along with George Thomas (now Viscount Tonypandy) and Gerald Williams, the sports commentator. (A later campaign in Northern Ireland featured Glenn Hoddle, Dana and myself.)

I just wish, as I say, that the church had been more alert to exploiting the publicity more fully, although, with hindsight, perhaps the American foundation was partly to blame for not gearing everyone up a few months beforehand. It's a bit too much to expect us to digest a whole new communications strategy over toast and marmalade first thing in the morning!

Incidentally, for me personally, what a great example that was of how God will ask a little and give back so much more. 'God is no man's debtor,' says the Bible, and, I tell you, that particular episode cost me absolutely nothing. Although the cynics will find it hard to swallow, I never contemplated any personal publicity angle whatsoever from the campaign. Our only criterion in accepting the invitation was whether it was right and worthwhile spiritually. But once the advertising was under way I realised how fantastic it was for me from a professional career point of view. A record company's sophisticated promotion machine could never have given me the high profile that the *Power For Living* campaign provided, and it was a lovely reminder of God's promise to Samuel: 'He who honours me, I will honour'.

It underlined too the fact that God's blessing isn't limited to some rarefied spiritual realm. He is as interested in what I get up to at the theatre on Monday as in what I do at church on Sunday, and he's at home in both places just the same.

Anyway, back to what's most important, and I'm conscious it's so easy to be glib. In fact the newspaper ad put it in a nutshell. Of course music, career, family, relationships, friends and tennis are all important to me in different ways and for different reasons, but behind the day's practical agenda, as it were, there's a reason and cohesion – something, if you like, that makes sense of all the work, relaxation and interests, and ensures that everything retains its proper perspective. That something, as you know, is my relationship with God. And because that has implications for literally everything I do – every song I sing, every script I undertake, every human relationship that develops, every decision about allocating time – it has to be what is ultimately most important.

It doesn't mean I'm obsessed or have become some creepy religious nut. I don't spend all day humming hymn tunes or spouting religious jargon. Nor do I buttonhole total strangers – or anyone, come to that – and ask them embarrassing questions about being saved. Although, for a gimmick, I once walked down Oxford Street with a sandwich-board advertising a Tearcraft exhibition at a nearby church hall. I admit it was dark, and I did walk quickly!

Let me put it like this. Simply by acknowledging God as life's focal point, every strand of activity has to relate in some way to him. And by 'acknowledging God' I don't mean just a grudging admission that he exists. (According to polls, the majority of British people would do that, yet there's no way we can call ourselves a Christian country.) I mean acknowledging that this is God's world, that he is active in it, and that, so far as I'm concerned, because in the mid-Sixties I seriously invited Him to take control of my life, he actually lives by his spirit within me and enables me to be just a fraction more like the person he intended. 'Power For Living' – just that.

Of course you're entitled to be cynical, and every day I do get it wrong – often badly wrong. But God doesn't keep a score-board of pluses and minuses, and when it came to the crunch soon after my conversion I proved, to myself at least, that he really did have first place. The chief contender for the throne was and still is, I suppose, my career. If one had to go, which would it be – my faith or the job I love? I wrote about it in 1977 in my autobiography *Which One's Cliff?* and I called the chapter 'My Little Isaac'.

The only thing I'd ever wanted to do was to sing and be a rock star. Yet, after becoming a Christian, I felt compelled to chuck it all in. I didn't understand how God could use me as an entertainer, so I dismantled my fan club, sat an 'O' level in RE, and talked with the principal of a teacher training college. I thought that teaching would be a useful kind of alternative. It was only when I'd made up my mind and put the wheels in motion that God held back the sacrificial knife, so to speak, and said, 'Wait a minute, I don't really need that.' Not a voice in the ear, I hasten to add, but via a totally unexpected set of circumstances which changed my thinking and opened up a whole new career dimension.

As I say, that was a long time ago, but I know that, so far as I'm concerned, nothing has changed. If I believed tomorrow that God wanted me to quit show business, I'd be out in the time it took to cancel contracts. That may not convince you, but *I'm* sure of it. OK, I would miss the money and the thrill of entertaining a huge crowd and the challenge of keeping up with new studio technology and the hundred-and-one other perks and privileges of being a so-called star. But I'd know that if God wanted me out he'd have something far better in store, for I've long since discovered that it isn't God's way to cramp your style or frustrate your ambitions. Quite the opposite – he's very much about expansion and development!

I guess I'd better not gloss over the money factor quite that simply, for I'm well aware it is potentially our most demanding twentieth-century idol, and you bet I'd miss it. I've got used to eating out in good restaurants and paying over the odds in exclusive men's shops. I don't have worries about switching on the central heating for an extra couple of hours or talking for thirty minutes on a long-distance telephone call. If I fancy a weekend in the sun (which is often) and work schedules permit (which is rare), I can nip off to my villa in Portugal without checking the house-keeping. I'd be a liar if I pretended that money didn't matter, and if my income dried up overnight and my investments crumbled I honestly don't know how hard a blow it would be.

I'd certainly be forced to make radical lifestyle changes, and I'd have to find a cheaper tennis club, but how destroyed would I be in the process? Could I let go of it all without bitterness and complaint? Until it happened I'd never know for sure, but I think I could.

For a start, I've been through the poverty experience and, although I was only a kid at the time, I remember it well enough to know that, despite very real hardship, we were united and happy as a family. Having wealth later on didn't make us any happier. It made life more comfortable, right enough. It increased our security and removed all sorts of anxieties, but it did nothing to improve relationships, deepen friendships or, if it doesn't sound too much of a cliché, provide that vital 'inner peace' which is so elusive. So I know that the wealth and happiness equation is a delusion.

Secondly, I know myself well enough to be satisfied that material things aren't that great an influence. A while back a burglar broke into my house and stole a number of valuable rings and watches from my bedroom. I can remember only two emotions. One was anger that someone should think he had the right to take what wasn't his, and the other was sadness at losing a ring that was given to me by Mamie, who had died a few months before.

In all honesty, I felt totally indifferent about losing the rest. And, without wanting to sound too good to be true, I reckon I'm just as philosophical when it comes to dropping the prize china or pranging the car. Even when it's some other twit who does it, I never feel particularly hung up or distraught.

Obviously accidents like that may be inconvenient, disappointing and downright expensive, but I can't think of any one thing that would devastate me if I lost it, broke it or had it stolen. And that's the key to it. 'Where your treasure is, there your heart will be also.'

Now I wouldn't claim that my heart is always where God directed it should be, but I am confident that he has a much larger share of it than any possession, bank account or blue chip investment, or whatever the phrase is. And being fairly at peace with myself in that respect, I find no contradiction in having wealth and being a Christian. Sure, I enjoy the freedom and the opportunities that material resources bring, but that is biblical. 'God . . . provides us with everything for our enjoyment', we're told. Nothing killjoy about that.

But not so easy to the ear is the other principle that 'From everyone who has been given much, much will be required', because their responsibility is greater. For me, as for all of us, it's a matter of balance. It isn't what we have, it's how we use it; not what we spend, but what we spend it on. And that, it seems to me, is a very personal and private matter.

It's an open secret that the work of *Tear Fund* in needy areas around the world has had my practical support for many years. The more I've seen of *Tear Fund*'s ways of working in places like Haiti, Sudan, Kenya and Bangladesh, the more deeply committed I've become, and I'm proud of the fact that our annual gospel concert tours in the UK have to date raised something approaching half a million pounds for all sorts of development projects.

If my memory serves me right, it was in the late Sixties that I first got involved, and from concert stages ever since I've been urging people to support and to give. Very many of my fans have done just that, and have discovered with me that *Tear Fund* and all it stands for in terms of Christian love in action has given back by way of personal challenge, satisfaction and encouragement far more than they have ever given.

If I've 'grown up' at all as a Christian, then *Tear Fund* has certainly played its part in the process, and I look back on my Third World trips not with distaste, but with immense appreciation.

At the time of writing we are throwing around more ideas for the future, including the possibility of shooting a thirty-minute music video in locations from Latin America to Asia, letting the pictures and the lyrics tell their own story.

What has become deeply embedded in my approach is the importance of long-term ongoing aid as opposed to the one-off blitz; and, if I have any reservations at all about the massively successful *Live Aid/Band Aid* events of the mid-Eighties, it was their 'one-off' nature. There was a danger, it seemed to me, that those who supported those events may have felt that they had 'done their bit', and I wonder how many of the kids who enjoyed that historic day in the sunshine at Wembley Stadium learnt anything about a continuing personal responsibility to give and to be involved.

To be fair, it probably wasn't the organisers' intention to educate; the objective was to raise money, and that they certainly did – fifty million pounds or more, which has been well and responsibly used. For once I felt quite a pride in our rock industry, which is renowned more for its taking than for its giving. But even fifty million pounds is a drop in the bucket when it comes to a world where two-thirds of its population are desperately deprived in one way or another. And it's necessary to raise it again this year, and the year after, and the year after that.

Somehow I wish that Bob Geldof, who gave himself so

tirelessly and wonderfully to the task, had stirred up a more constructive motive to give than guilt. 'If you haven't pledged your gift yet, you ought to be ashamed of yourself.' It was a real sledge-hammer approach, and was fine if the aim was for people to donate just once. But if the hope was for sustained public generosity, I believe motivation should have been generated at a much deeper level.

It was years ago that I discovered the most healthy reason to give is not because you're bludgeoned into it or because you've been made to feel a right heel, but because you're genuinely grateful for what you have. That's at the heart of the Christian gospel, which replaces destructive guilt with practical and outgoing love and appreciation.

The one accolade which in my book Bob Geldof never did deserve was the newspaper headline that announced, 'Sinner Geldof Does More Than All The Churches Put Together.' Purely in terms of cash raised for a specific need, that's probably true – but then the churches don't have the resources of a wealthy industry to draw on. Measured against the commitment of countless individuals, however, the headline is unfair and misleading, and, knowing Bob as I do, I'm positive he would be the first to say so.

Bob did a magnificent job, but how do you compare it, say, to the work of the ageing spinster missionary who's been caring for children on the island of La Gonave off Haiti for more years than Bob has been living? That is the church's response to practical need. So is the work of Mother Theresa in Calcutta, who says she cares for the sick and the dying because she 'loves Jesus'. So is the sacrificial month-by-month giving by countless numbers of 'ordinary' Christians in Britain, whose generosity doesn't dry up when the publicity dies down. To write off the church's expression of practical caring as flippantly as that headline is prejudiced and dishonest.

Bob's effort was outstanding, that's for sure, but we would do well to save our best superlatives for the givers at home who don't need the armlock, and for the hordes of nurses and teachers, engineers and doctors, mechanics and builders who never attract the headlines, but who are out at the sharp end, sometimes literally putting their lives on the line for years at a time for no other reason than a love of their neighbour. Not all of them are Christians, I hasten to add, because Christianity doesn't have a monopoly on goodness, but a hefty proportion are, and they're involved simply because their faith allows no option. It is the Christian's responsibility to love; it's his trademark, if you like, and without it faith is phoney and a mockery.

Perhaps society needs its Bob Geldofs from time to time to prick its humanitarian conscience and goad it into action, but more than that society needs its Christian evangelists and teachers, its Billy Grahams and its John Stotts, who can proclaim and spell out how the individual can be changed from within and produce the fruit of compassion, love and generosity without the threats and the cajoling.

The Christian nurse in the Ethiopian refugee camp, for instance, is there only because five years ago she gave her life to Christ at a local evangelistic rally. Since then her priorities have changed. She has a new concern for God's world and a new desire to do his will at whatever personal cost. And the Christian family who need to budget carefully to make ends meet have a standing order with their bank so that, come what may, a monthly gift is earmarked for the relief agency. They've learnt the principle of being responsible stewards of what God has given them.

St Paul's comparison of the church to the human body was a clever one. Just as all the parts of the body need each other to function properly and efficiently, so does the church. We all have different gifts and talents, but it's pointless to say that one is more important than the other.

One of the sharpest retorts I ever received was from a nurse in Bangladesh who, after a harrowing day in one of the refugee camps, heard me express reluctance about going back to the UK. Somehow I felt I was opting out of what I saw as real commitment and, compared to those nurses, was doing precious little of real importance. I wanted to get *my* hands dirty too. 'Can you give an injection?' the nurse interrupted. 'No way,' I said. 'I'd never have the nerve.' 'Then go home. We don't need you here,' she said. 'Go back and do what you're good at.'

That was a long time ago, but it's a lesson I've never forgotten. Since then I've neither underestimated my role in God's kingdom, nor thought less about anyone else's.

It's best not to fret over whether our life's efforts seem important. Who's to say and who's to judge? More to the point is whether we're sure those efforts are pleasing to God – assuming of course that he is where our treasure is!

10 WHEN IT'S TIME TO QUIT

10 WHEN IT'S TIME TO QUIT

There are times, I have to admit, when I wish I could jack it all in next week. The prospect of waking up in the morning with the day to myself would be sheer bliss. No autographs, no interviews, no rehearsal calls – I drool at the thought! Friends tell me I'd be bored out of my skull within a month, but they're wrong. Perhaps they interpret retirement as doing nothing, but that's not what I have in mind.

Certainly there's no way I could sit around and twiddle my thumbs for days on end, and I just can't imagine what life must be like with literally nothing to occupy the hours. Retirement for me would simply mean doing something different, and probably exchanging one hectic schedule for another. It's merely that sometimes I long to be in a situation where there are simply no demands, and I guess all of us daydream about that when life tends to get on top of us.

Realistically, and on less pressurised days (and this may relieve or depress you!), retirement isn't an option I've seriously considered. I'd like to think that the diary will move out of overdrive to allow at least one free day a week, particularly after I hit the big Five-O (management, please note!). But, all things considered, I've no plans for any farewell concert – although the thought of singing 'Miss You Nights' for the last time, to the accompaniment of a few thousand rustling tissues, does have a certain dramatic appeal!

Rightly or wrongly, I believe I still have something to offer – and, arrogant though it sounds, I still think I can sing as well as anybody in the business. The challenge for me is to prove it by making records that sell, and that's the rub! There's no way I've ever taken popularity for granted, and the idea that records sell purely on the strength of a name or reputation is a fallacy. If your work doesn't please people it won't sell, and that's true for any artist. So far I've been fortunate in that my tastes have coincided with those of my fans, and if I can maintain that sensitivity and keep the voice in reasonably good order, then there's no need to apply for a pension book just yet!

If musical styles had radically changed, it might be different. Perhaps I'd have got left behind. But rock 'n' roll is essentially the same. It's grown up a good deal, that's for sure, but it hasn't intrinsically altered. Today's young solo artists (such as Paul Young, Nik Kershaw, George Michael, and so on) aren't singing that differently, they're just very good at what they do. And it's those of us who are a bit further down the road – the likes of myself, Elton John, Mick Jagger and David Bowie – who've been at it for twenty-five or thirty years, who are proving that, far from being a monopoly of the young, rock 'n' roll has effectively spanned the generation gap and is here to stay as an acceptable art form.

Who would have thought that those mohair-suited, lip-curling kids of the *Oh Boy!* and *Six Five Special* days would still be loving their rock 'n' roll at fifty, and that the punters, every bit as dedicated, would be setting them up to be the Frank Sinatras of their generation? And there's no way that prospect saddens or depresses me. If I can sing as well at sixty as Sinatra did at seventy, and get the same reaction, who's to complain?

What I could never face would be a slow but steady decline. A couple of years ago, I was in Bristol and spotted a blackboard in the entrance of a very ordinary hotel. Scrawled in chalk was the forthcoming attraction – someone who during the Sixties was a really big name and notched up a whole string of chart hits. I could never imagine playing in a place like that. Maybe I'm too spoilt, or my ego couldn't cope, but frankly I'm not that desperate for an audience!

As far as I can see right now, there are only three factors that would cause me to duck out. Obviously if my voice cracked up and I couldn't do it, I'd have no choice. Secondly if I released four or five records which made little or no impression on the market, I'd take that as a fair indication that I'd lost touch with public taste. Thirdly, I'd quit if I got bored, because there's no way you can pretend for long. Fans know if you're jaded and merely going through the motions, and, quite rightly, they'll lose interest mighty fast.

Elton was wise to pull out for a couple of years at exactly the right time. He admitted he'd lost interest in performing, but instead of waiting for audiences to dwindle, which they surely would have done, he took the early initiative and sprang the bombshell which dismayed admirers around the world. We all know that Elton came back rejuvenated after his lay-off, and he's bigger now than ever before. I suspect it would have been a different story if he'd hung about and infected his fans with his own boredom. Their 'Welcome Back' would have been far less ecstatic.

For me the perfect recipe for the next ten, twenty or however many years that remain would contain a whole variety of ingredients. Gone are the days when I'd be happy just to tour or just to record or just to perform. I'm still as enthusiastic about all three, but also about much more besides.

My year in *Time*, for instance, opened up a whole new vista for me, and the urge to be involved in future West End shows is really strong. For a start, there's a huge potential market – remember that during those twelve months at the Dominion Theatre we played to getting on for three-quarters of a million people. I wouldn't be greatly fussed about the kind of show I did next, although it would be fantastic to do another rock 'n' roll musical. But a passing remark by Jeff Shankley, the actor who played Melchisedic in *Time*, has taken root in my mind. If I didn't know him so well, I wouldn't be sure how to take it, but he said I'd be great in a farce! According to him, my stage timing was good, and comedy would be a natural vehicle.

I don't know about the comedy, but if the chance cropped up to do an original play, farce or otherwise, with a bunch of experienced actors, I'm sure I could hold up my end of it. But I'd need those other actors. We rock 'n' roll singers tend to think we can do anything on stage, because our careers have thrown us high. In fact I try to keep a tight rein on my ego in that particular area. I've worked with actors, and I know that most of them are in a different league to me when it comes to getting inside another character. The secret is to ensure that what I have to offer is wrapped up with other people who know the rules of acting better than I do.

But the encouragement that I'll treasure for the rest of my life was from none other than Laurence Olivier himself. After he'd watched a matinée performance of *Time* from the

Royal Circle, he came backstage and took me to one side. 'My boy,' he said in that gentle but authoritative voice, 'one of these days you're going to be big in the West End.' I daren't ask in what particular capacity, but I was walking on air for a week!

And then there's America – still the biggest record outlet of all, still beckoning, and still a major cause of frustration. For me it's the final frontier, and the one remaining ambition of my pop career is to crack it. Forget the finance and the royalties and the possible sales figures – they have nothing to do with it. I've got all I need, and more, from the rest of the world. It's purely and simply a matter of personal satisfaction and achievement.

Here I am, having spent more time in the UK charts than any other artist (The Beatles included) – with the sole exception of Elvis – yet the average American will never have heard of me. He or she'll probably recognise a song title – 'Devil Woman', 'We Don't Talk Any More', 'Dreamin'', 'Daddy's Home' and others were all decent-sized Top Thirty hits over the years. But as for Cliff Richard, the name won't mean a light.

Why that is, I'm really not sure. Perhaps my record company has never worked at projecting any personal image and has assumed that success in the rest of the world was enough to get me across. Maybe I haven't set enough time to be seen and heard on the media, or to be available for those endless 'personal appearances' that Americans love and seem to demand. 'Out of sight, out of mind,' really is true. Maybe, I have to tell myself, they just don't like what I do. Whatever the reason, and despite the fact that the industry itself invites me to take on high-calibre TV shows such as their *Top of the Pops* equivalent *Solid Gold*, America still eludes me, and that's a challenge.

Who knows, by the time you read this I may have had a major chart success and recognition will have dawned overnight. If it happens, though, and if I have anything to do with it, you can be sure it will be on my terms. I've never had to tout around for favours and I don't intend to start now. Nor would I ever sell my soul to Las Vegas or the night-club circuit, however lucrative. That's never been my scene, and I can't imagine anything changing now.

If the breakthrough does occur, it will be because I've made a record that has that magic American ingredient,

and the record company will have at last effectively packaged and sold Cliff Richard. I'd be thrilled, if only to say I'd
made it in the fatherland of rock 'n' roll!

Amazingly enough, I do have a fan club in the States. It's
tiny, and you could probably pack all the members into a
telephone box, but the important thing is that it exists –
and, I tell you, to be a Cliff fan there means real dedication.
I'm all the more grateful for their support and constant
entreaties to visit. Sometimes, I know, I've upset them by
seeming to 'knock' their country, but although admittedly
I'm particularly critical of some parts of the music industry,
it really isn't vindictive criticism.

Basically what gives me trouble is the blatant success
orientation. I've visited when I've had a song in the charts
and I've visited when action is zero. The difference in the
way I'm received is nauseating. People should be important
irrespective of status, and I find it disconcerting when
success is apparently the sole criterion for serious attention.
I know it's easy to misconstrue that as sour grapes, but
those who know me well acknowledge that I couldn't care
less about shiny limos at airports and being fêted at ritzy
receptions. What counts for me is that people are real and
consistent, and I'd gladly exchange the limos, receptions
and all the other superficial gloss for a genuinely workmanlike and professional relationship with a record company
that demonstrates its commitment; not just with candy-
floss when I'm around, but with initiative when I'm not.

In many ways I have a love/hate relationship with the US.
Ambivalent, I think the word is. New York and Los Angeles
are exciting vibrant places that pump the adrenalin and
seem to work up irrational levels of expectation. But,
whereas I love to visit, I could never contemplate living in
an environment where showbiz seems to have escaped
from its proper confines and influenced regular workaday
life. Showbiz is about fantasy, make-believe and escapism.
That's great on stage, but disturbing and downright
dangerous in the High Street!

Record production is something else I'd like more time to
pursue. Over the years I've produced albums for Christian
artists such as Dave Pope, Garth Hewitt and Sheila Walsh,
but they've been isolated projects and somehow always
crammed into gaps in my own mad schedule as 'favours'
for friends.

I've tried my hand at producing some of my own tracks, but the problem there is that it's hard not to be self-indulgent and even harder to stay really critically objective. But I enjoy the responsibility and creative challenge of production, and feel that, given enough elbow room and a period of uncluttered time, I have sufficient studio know-how to get good results. After all, fifty or so albums and a hundred singles of my own, and a career charging towards its fourth decade, ought to have taught me something, and I'd be a bit of a wally if I couldn't draw on it.

Perhaps it's moving into daydream time to think of management and steering someone else's career. Theoretically I'd love to take it on, and I'd get enormous satisfaction from discovering some unknown talent and taking him or her through the industry minefield to international success and acclaim. But it could only work if I'd turned my back once and for all on being an artist myself. There's no way I could run someone else's career and have my own ticking over in the background. Ours is an industry where it's every man for himself, and if I found a great song and I was still recording, my protégé would stand as much chance of getting it as of me going heavy metal. Not exactly a sound basis for upright management!

I'm a bit doubtful, too, about handling the admin. Decisions are no problem. I'm good at doing what's right for me, and that means deciding almost daily whether to accept or reject the advice of others, and I do both and I don't dither. In that respect I'd be a businesslike business man. But admin. – that's something else. If management means reading – let alone writing – letters and keeping accounts and remembering appointments and understanding contracts, and I suspect it does (plus a bit more besides), then sadly I'll have to pass. A worse nightmare would be hard to imagine!

Then again there's filming. 'Why not another *Summer Holiday* or *Young Ones*?', I'm always asked. After all, they were smash successes of their own day and I was twice voted 'Box Office Draw of the Year'. So, yes, I'd leap at the chance of another movie. I'd approach it with much greater maturity, that's for sure – and, I'd like to think, with vastly improved acting ability. But film parts aren't exactly two a penny, so, to be realistic, I can't imagine film-makers queuing up to offer me plum roles.

Long gone are the days when *Summer Holiday* and the like could be made for relatively modest budgets and have a fair chance of making money. Today major movie budgets run into many millions, and the stakes are precariously high. What casting director is seriously going to consider a rock 'n' roll singer whose acting credentials would barely qualify him for a part in *Neighbours*?

If personal confidence were anything to go by, I'd be on the first plane out to Hollywood. As it is, I'll continue to turn down the B-movie rubbish, of which there's no particular shortage, and cling optimistically to the hope that some day a Spielberg or a Puttnam will be on the phone to request a meeting. I'm not fussy about the part, just so long as there are no red buses!

To be serious, I'm convinced there's marvellous dramatic potential in the true-life stories of men such as Hudson Taylor or William Carey. OK, they're Christian missionaries, and that means immediate prejudice and wrong assumptions, but read the stories. Their lives reflect an incredible gamut of emotion, conflict and adventure, and in my opinion would translate into riveting cinema. If there's a film-maker with vision enough to consider it and backing enough to tackle it, then say the word and you've got me! And I'm very cheap!

One area where I feel I should exert more effort is song-writing. I feel almost guilty that I haven't come up with material more often, because when inspiration does get through the results really aren't bad. The problem is that I need to get motivated. In the early days, when I had a hand in writing things like 'Bachelor Boy', 'On The Beach' and 'Don't Talk To Him', there were the Shads around to spark off ideas, and it was natural to sit around in hotels and on tour buses, just messing about with guitar chords and the odd lyric.

Then came the *Tear Fund* visits to places like Bangladesh and Haiti, and they proved the stimulus for material that, to be honest, I'm quite proud of. I vividly remember standing at the prow of an old boat, chugging across from Haiti to an even poorer little island, when, in less than two hours, I'd got the song 'La Gonave' clearly in my head. It was a relief not to be seasick for a change.

But occasions like that, when everything is fresh and the emotions are so stirred, are relatively few, and most of the time there's neither the incentive nor those 'empty hours' to sit back and create. Maybe I lack the mental discipline to put my mind deliberately to writing, but the work schedule I've had for the past few years is alibi enough. Plus, the knowledge that fine writers such as Alan Tarney and Terry Britten let me record the cream of their output simply allows me to bask in their talent. There's no way I could compete with real genius, so I've geared myself to being an interpreter of songs rather than a singer-songwriter. Yet all the time there's the niggle that it might be different, and that deep inside lyrics and melodies could be struggling to get out. Perhaps in those heady relaxed days ahead there'll be the chance to find out.

So far the nearest I've ever got to a 'written and sung by' album was *The 31st of February Street*, back in the early Seventies. There must have been a rush of blood to the head around that period, because no less than four tracks on the album were mine. No wonder it didn't sell too well!

I've only myself to blame, I know, but I do begrudge the lack of quality 'thinking time'. Too often I seem to be caught up in that 'constant rush' syndrome, and that's when the thought of retirement becomes enticing. So far the pressure always seems to ease just before the fuse blows, but, as early middle age creaks discreetly into rather later middle age, I suspect that detonation time may be that much closer. It's not that there's anything particularly profound which I'm dying to resolve. It's just that sometimes it's good to let your mind focus on things other than work, and the only occasion I've had that luxury was again in the early Seventies, when somehow I contrived to spend a whole term sharing a pew with trainee clergy at a theological college.

In a public garden near the Norfolk Broads, there's an old well-worn seat with a plaque inviting passers-by to 'Sit ye down and mardle awhile'. I've never been sure what mardling is exactly, but it's a great word and sounds exactly what I mean. I can't wait to do a bit more mardling, and I only hope it isn't rude!

The truth is that, outside of my career, I don't have any burning ambitions. Sure, when I'm seventy I want to be able to thrash every other seventy-year-old upstart off the tennis court. That goes without saying. But there's no frustrated politician or street campaigner longing for a chance to go public. I never have been a campaigner as such, and I have to own up to a certain cynicism towards the protest-marcher, who aggressively stands out against one social problem while deliberately contributing to another.

Although I've become far more alert to political issues and have even found myself getting quite steamed up over certain attitudes that have emerged in our society over recent years, I've no desire whatever to tread any party political path. I'm clear about where to cast my personal vote, but there's no way I'd want to influence or persuade anyone else. In an ideal world I guess our common concern would be for the good of the nation as a whole, and self-interest would be irrelevant as to where we put our cross, but it isn't like that. We vote for whoever we reckon will best feather our own nests, and, although I suppose that's how it has to be, I find the whole business just a tiny bit disconcerting.

For me the one realistic personal ideal is to allow Christ to sort out my life as only he can, and then let it filter into the lives of others, hoping it can be of some value. That means, if and when I have more time on my hands, it will be automatic to devote some to specifically Christian activity.

I've no idea exactly how many invitations I have to turn down at present to take part in really worthwhile Christian communication around the world, but I know it is the relative exception that finds its way into the diary. Maybe one day that will change and there will be opportunity to do more. I hope so, not because I fancy myself as a Billy Graham or a John Stott, but because I can be a fair old Cliff Richard, and I'm happy to settle for that. Thankfully God doesn't put any pressure on any of us, myself included, to be like somebody else, however great and admirable. He wants us to be ourselves, no more and no less. Call it a cop-out, if you like, but the nearest I get to the proverbial burning ambition is to be as good as I can be at what I am.

If past books are anything to go by, there may be some readers who'd like to explore more about the Christian faith. You will understand, I'm sure, that it's impossible for me to reply to enquiries personally, but I have a great group of Christian friends who would be really glad to help – and they probably know far more than I do anyway! You can contact them at the following address: PO Box 79C, Esher, Surrey, KT10 9LP.